handy homework helper

U.S. History

Writers:
Susan Bloom
Maggie Ronzani

Consultant:
Linda Symcox

Publications International, Ltd.

Copyright © 1997 Publications International, Ltd. All rights reserved. This book may not be reproduced or quoted in whole or in part by any means whatsoever without written permission from:

Louis Weber, C.E.O.
Publications International, Ltd.
7373 North Cicero Avenue
Lincolnwood, Illinois 60646

Permission is never granted for commercial purposes.

Manufactured in China.

8 7 6 5 4 3 2 1

ISBN: 0-7853-1952-2

Susan Bloom is a freelance writer and editor with Creative Services Associates, Inc., a publisher of educational materials for over 15 years. She has taught composition and literature at a community college for 15 years and holds a B.S. in English from Southern Methodist University and an M.A. in English from the University of California-Los Angeles.

Maggie Ronzani is a writer and editor with Creative Services Associates, Inc., a publisher of educational materials for over 15 years. She has over 25 years experience in educational publishing and has an A.B. in English from Creighton University in Omaha and an M.B.A. in Marketing from DePaul University in Chicago.

Linda Symcox was the Associate Director for the National Center for History in the Schools, University of California, Los Angeles, and edited the National History Standards. She has consulted and written numerous publications, including *World History The Easy Way, Vol. I*, and *America: Pathways To The Present*. She is a member of the American Historical Association and the National Council for History Education.

Photo Research: Joyce Stirniman/Creative Services Associates, Inc.

Cover photography: Siede Preis Photography

Models and agencies: Royal Modeling Management: Dustin Berman, Roger Kung, Chesney Melissa Murphy, Cerena Olsen, Billy Pyroulis, Alanna Jasmine Ramirez.

Photo credits: AP/Wide World Photos, Inc.: 99 (left), 106, 107, 111 (top & bottom), 112, 114 (top), 115 (top), 120 (top); Ron Edmonds: contents (bottom left), 122 (top); **Archive Photos:** 15 (top left), 16 (bottom), 20 (top), 23, 25 (top left), 31 (bottom), 34 (top), 37 (center & bottom left), 55, 57, 60, 61, 66, 67 (bottom), 74 (bottom), 76 (left), 78, 79 (bottom), 82 (top), 83, 84, 89 (top & bottom), 93 (top & left center), 94 (top), 96, 101 (bottom), 104 (top), 111 (center), 116 (center & top), 119 (bottom), 120 (bottom); AgenceFrance-Presse: 113 (top); David Brauchli/ Reuthers: 121; Corinne Dufka/Reuthers: 122 (bottom right); Express Newspapers: 119 (top); Hirz: 90 (top); Lambert: 26, 33; Museum of the City of New York: 91 (center), 94 (bottom); Potter Collection: 110 (top); **Art Resource, NY:** National Museum of American Art, Washington, DC: 68 (bottom); National Portrait Gallery, Smithsonian Institution: contents (bottom right), 49, 71 (top), 82 (bottom), 95 (left), 108 (top); **Bettmann Archive:** 8, 10 (bottom), 11, 12 (top), 14, 16 (top), 20 (bottom), 28 (top), 30 (top), 42 (bottom), 44, 48 (top), 56, 59 (top), 69 (bottom), 72 (bottom), 74 (center), 75 (top), 92 (left), 109; Corbis: 10 (top), 21, 22 (bottom), 29 (bottom), 62, 65, 103 (bottom), 110 (bottom); **Bridgeman Art Library:** Bonhams, London: 67 (top); John Noott Galleries, Broadway, Worcs: 33 (top); Private Collection: 32; **Culver Pictures, Inc.:** 31 (top), 33 (center), 34 (center), 36, 39, 42 (top), 64, 71 (right), 76 (right), 81 (top), 91 (top & bottom), 93 (center & right center), 99 (right), 102, 103 (top), 104 (bottom); **FPG International:** 19, 29 (top), 59 (bottom), 72 (top), 81 (bottom), 86 (bottom), 88 (center), 95 (right), 98 (bottom), 101 (top), 108 (bottom), 114 (bottom); Ron Chapple: 117 (bottom); John Senser: 7; J. Sylvester: 50; **Bill Stanton/International Stock:** 122 (bottom left); **Stock Montage, Inc.:** 105; **Superstock:** contents (top left), 6 (top & bottom left), 12 (bottom), 18, 22 (top), 24, 25 (top right), 27, 28 (bottom), 34 (bottom), 40 (bottom), 43, 48 (bottom), 52, 54, 68 (top), 69 (top), 70, 74 (top), 75 (bottom), 77, 80, 86 (top), 88 (top & bottom), 89 (center), 90 (bottom), 92 (right), 98 (top & center), 103 (center), 113 (bottom), 115 (bottom), 116 (bottom), 117 (top); Antochiw Collection: 15 (center); Michael J. Lowell: 6 (bottom center); Metropolitan Museum of Art, New York City: contents (top right), 46; Private Collection: 79 (top); **White Eagle Studios:** 76 (bottom).

Map Illustrations: Thomas Cranmer.

Spot Illustrations: Anita Nelson.

Photo Tinting Artist: Cheryl Winser.

Contents

About This Book

Homework takes time and a lot of hard work. Many students would say it's their least favorite part of the school day. But it's also one of the most important parts of your school career because it does so much to help you learn. Learning gives you knowledge, and knowledge gives you power.

Homework gives you a chance to review the material you've been studying so you understand it better. It lets you work on your own, which can give you confidence and independence. Doing school work at home also gives your parents a way to find out what you're studying in school.

Everyone has trouble with their homework from time to time, and *Handy Homework Helper: U.S. History* can help you when you run into a problem. This book was prepared with the help of educational specialists. It offers quick, simple explanations of the basic material that you're studying in school. If you get stuck on an idea or have trouble finding some information, *Handy Homework Helper: U.S. History* can help clear it up for you. It can also help your parents help you by giving them a fast refresher course in the subject.

This book is clearly organized by the topics you'll be studying in U.S. History. A quick look at the Table of Contents will tell you which chapter covers the area you're working on. You can probably guess which chapter includes what you need and then flip through the chapter until you find it. For even more help finding what you're looking for, look up key words related to what you're studying in the Index. You might find material faster that way, and you might also find useful information in a place you wouldn't have thought to look.

Remember that different teachers and different schools take different approaches to teaching History. For that reason, we recommend that you talk with your teacher about using this homework guide. You might even let your teacher look through the book so he or she can help you use it in a way that best matches what you're studying at school.

American Beginnings

Prehistory

The United States is a young nation. Yet, people have lived on American lands for more than 20,000 years. Around that time, the earth was going through an ice age. Huge sheets of ice covered most of the northern half of the planet, and the level of the oceans was lower. Land that is now underwater was exposed. Part of the Bering Strait, which is the body of water between Russia and Alaska, was above sea level and formed a bridge between the two lands. Asian hunters following animals crossed the bridge and spread throughout the Americas. They were the first Americans. Eventually, people were living everywhere from the northern regions of North America to the southern tip of South America.

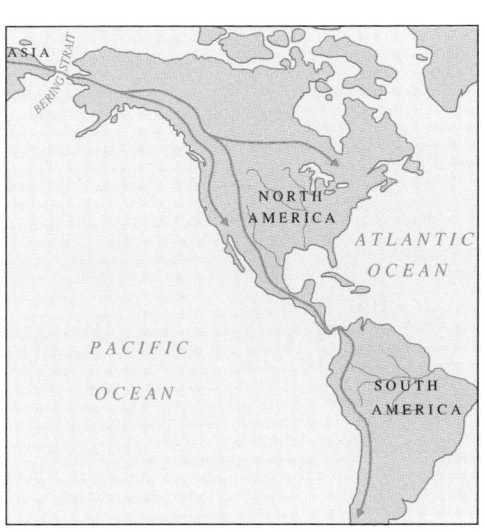

HUMAN MIGRATION ACROSS THE BERING STRAIT

The first Americans led a wandering life in search of food. Later, some groups began to farm. Indians in Mexico began farming cereal crops like wheat and corn about 7000 B.C. This meant they could live in one place, form villages, and do work other than finding food. Many different civilizations and cultures sprang up in North America and South America.

First people spread across North America

20,000 B.C.

7000 B.C.

People begin farming in the Americas

Early American Cultures

The Indians in America had many different ways of life. Some groups are known from the big mounds of earth they built that still remain today. As early as 1000 B.C., people built mounds to use as burial grounds, worship places, and sites for leaders' homes. Three main **mound builder** cultures were the Adena, the Hopewell, and the Mississippian.

The Adenas lived in what is now Ohio from 1000 B.C. until A.D. 200. They built some mounds in striking shapes, such as the Great Serpent mound near Hillsboro, Ohio. Shaped like a snake, it is ¼ mile (.4 km) long. The Adenas lived in small villages. They lived mostly by hunting, fishing, and gathering.

The Great Serpent mound built by the Adenas is now part of a state park in Ohio.

The Hopewells were farmers of crops such as corn and squash. They lived in what is now Ohio, Indiana, Michigan, Illinois, Wisconsin, Iowa, and Missouri from about 100 B.C. until about A.D. 500. Both the Adenas and the Hopewells put objects in the tombs they built. They felt that a person's spirit would use pipes, jewelry, pottery, and weapons in the next world.

The Mississippian culture built a city in what is now Illinois. They named it Cahokia, and at one point, 40,000 people lived there. That means Cahokia was as large as the modern cities of Palm Springs, California; Wheeling, West Virginia; Butte, Montana; and Bismark, North Dakota. Cahokia's largest mound covers about 16 acres (6 hectares). Goods found in

Olmec culture flourishes

Mogollon culture develops

1200 B.C.   **1000 B.C.**   **500 B.C.**   **100 B.C.**

Mound-building Adenas appear

Hopewell culture develops

The Anasazis left their cliff dwellings in the 1300s. They may have moved southwest to escape a long drought or warring neighbors.

the mounds show that the Mississippians traded with many of their neighbors.

In what is now the southwestern United States, people known as **cliff dwellers** built shelters in canyon walls and under over-hanging rock formations. The Anasazis lived between A.D. 1000 and 1300 in what is now Arizona, New Mexico, Utah, and Colorado. They were hunters and farmers who lived in two-story or three-story houses built in cliff walls or on ledges. They used lad-ders to reach entrances on upper levels. The ladders were lowered for residents and raised if enemies approached.

Another Southwest culture was the Mogollon people. They built dams and terraces that helped with their farming. Mogollons lived in Arizona and New Mexico from about 500 B.C. to A.D. 1200. They produced the finest pottery made in North America north of Mexico. They often painted geometric designs in red and brown or black and white on their pottery.

Anasazi ruins often contain decorative art carvings or written pictographs that tell a story. The pictographs tell us much about how these people lived.

Mayas begin to flourish

Anasazis build cliff dwellings;
Vikings reach North America

Incan empire dominates western coast of South America

A.D. 300   A.D. 600   A.D. 1000   1300   1400

Mississippians establish Cahokia

Aztecs establish city of Tenochtitlán

Indians Before 1492

After Europeans brought horses to America, many Indians changed their way of life. For instance, few Indian groups relied on buffalo before 1492 because they were difficult to hunt. With horses, the Plains Indians were able to use buffalo as their main source of food, shelter, and clothing.

Millions of people lived in North America in the late 1400s. They lived in hundreds of **tribes** throughout the land. They had many different ways of life. Many tribes lived near one another and shared the same culture. They lived in regions called **culture areas** by scientists and historians.

The homes that Indians lived in depended on climate and resources in the environment. For example, some people on the Plains lived in tepees made of animal skins, and some people in the Northwest lived in wooden multifamily houses. In the East, the Iroquois made buildings called longhouses, in which several families lived. Other tribes built lodges covered with mud.

Indians lived in groups with their extended families: grandparents, aunts, uncles, and cousins. Often, families joined together in a **band**, a group of 20 to 300 people. Several bands formed a **tribe**, which is a large group of people in a particular area with the same way of life and customs.

The daily life of Indians was based on working for food, clothing, and shelter. Men usually hunted for food, and women usually gathered plants and farmed.

Indians usually hunted whatever game they could in their area: fish, wild birds, deer, and rabbit. Many Indian people also gathered berries, nuts, and roots. Some of them farmed, raising mostly beans, squash, and corn.

Indians enjoyed playing games. They had foot races and played forms of hockey and basketball. They invented a game of racquetball, which grew into the game of lacrosse. They also developed unique arts and crafts.

Most Indian tribes had ceremonies that reflected their religious beliefs. The Plains Indians celebrated a sun dance to offer thanks. They also held a buffalo dance to bring good fortune in hunting. Farming tribes held rain dances. Tribes in the East held a corn dance in honor of each summer's corn crop.

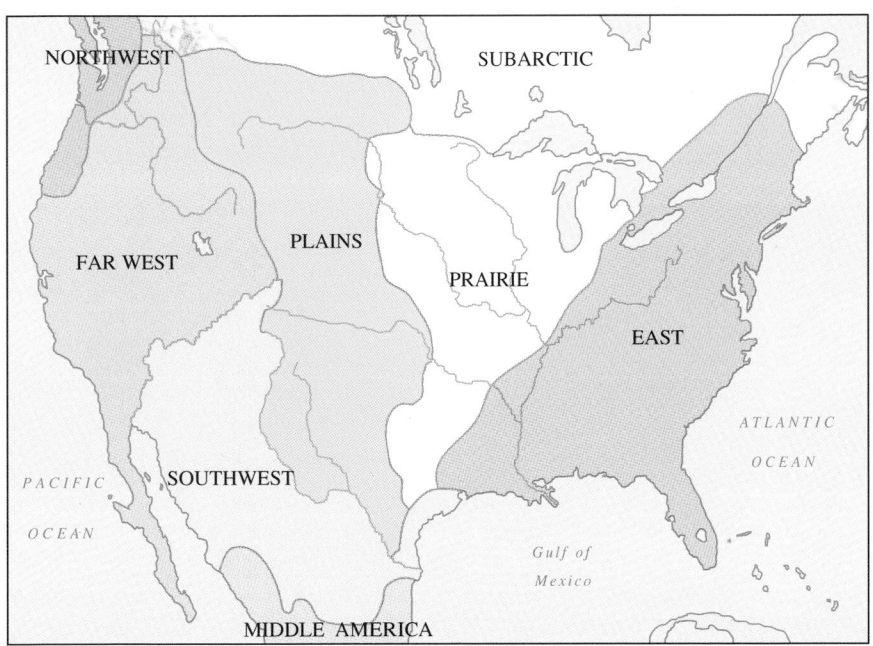

NORTH AMERICAN INDIAN CULTURE AREAS. The different tribes within a culture area shared the same lifestyle, but they often had different customs, religious beliefs, and languages. Some tribes would trade with each other, some would fight with each other, and some would do both.

In Search of the East

Henry the Navigator of Portugal watches as one of the expeditions he sponsored returns to port.

Trade with the Middle East

When Europeans began to travel to the Middle East, they were introduced to silk, spices, new jewels, and china. In 1095, Christian crusaders from Europe began a war against the Muslims in the Middle East. The crusaders wanted to control religious sites in the Middle East. They learned about the riches of African and Asian nations from Middle Eastern traders. They eagerly traded for the gold, spices, silk, and other goods from Asia and Africa.

Europeans became interested in Africa and in the Far East, which they called the **Indies**. In 1271, a young Italian named Marco Polo went to China. He wrote a book about his travels that increased European interest in the Asian countries.

Vasco da Gama prepares to set sail from Portugal in 1497 to find a water route to India.

By the 1400s, many Europeans wanted to trade directly with the Asians and avoid the cost of dealing with the Middle Eastern traders. However, the main trade routes were overland and were controlled by the Middle Easterners. This made the products from the Indies very expensive.

Chinese invent movable type

Marco Polo travels to China

1050　　　　**1095**　　　　　　　　　　　**1271**

The Crusades begin

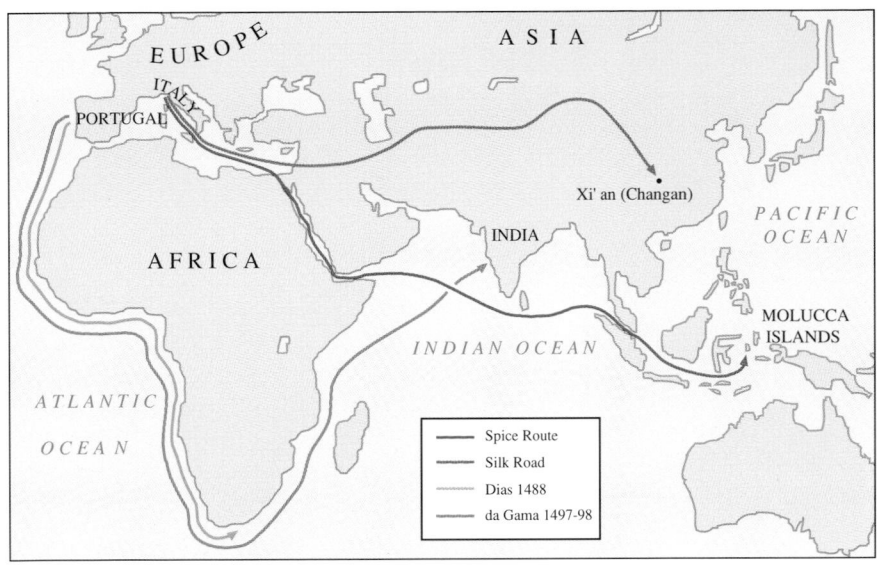

EUROPEAN TRAVEL TO THE FAR EAST, 15TH CENTURY

European explorers, especially those in Portugal and Spain, wanted to find a direct sea route to the Indies. The first Portuguese explorers tried to get to the east by sailing around the coast of Africa. Prince Henry, a son of the king of Portugal, sponsored many trips of exploration. He became known as Henry the Navigator.

A Portuguese explorer, Bartolomeu Dias, sailed around the southern tip of Africa in 1488. Vasco da Gama finally sailed around Africa and reached India in 1498.

These European explorers had new navigational tools to help them sail where they had not gone before. By checking the position of the sun and using an **astrolabe** and a **crossstaff**, they could determine their latitude. They also used a **compass**, an instrument invented in China.

16th century astrolabe

African slaves brought to Portugal

Bartolomeu Dias sails around the southern tip of Africa

| 1416 | 1440 | 1453 | 1488 |

Henry the Navigator sponsors trips along African coast

Johannes Gutenberg uses his printing press to print the Bible

Christopher Columbus

Christopher Columbus

A sailor named Christopher Columbus had a new idea of how to reach the Indies by water. Columbus believed that Japan was located 3,000 nautical miles (5,600 kilometers) west of Lisbon, Portugal. (It is actually 11,000 nautical miles—20,400 kilometers.) He thought he could sail west and reach the Indies.

In the 1480s, Columbus asked King John II of Portugal to sponsor an expedition west. The king refused. Later Columbus persuaded King Ferdinand and Queen Isabella of Spain to support his journey.

On August 3, 1492, Columbus left Palos, Spain, with three ships, the *Niña*, the *Pinta*, and the *Santa María*. They sailed to the Canary Islands and then headed west. On October 12, Columbus landed on San Salvador. He thought he had reached the Indies, and he called the people there Indians. Columbus left 40 sailors on the island of Haiti and returned to Spain with several Indians.

Columbus was welcomed as a hero. Ferdinand and Isabella wanted him to return to the islands to explore further. On his second trip, part of Columbus's crew colonized the island of Hispaniola. On Columbus's third trip, his ships landed on the coast of South America, and he was sure he had discovered a new continent. Columbus made his

Columbus and his crew are welcomed by natives as they arrive in the New World.

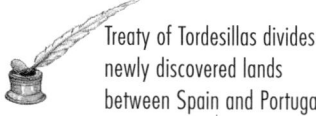

Treaty of Tordesillas divides newly discovered lands between Spain and Portugal

Vasco da Gama reaches India by sea

1492	1494	1497	1498	1500

Christopher Columbus reaches the Americas

John Cabot lands at Newfoundland

Pedro Alvares Cabral of Portugal claims Brazil

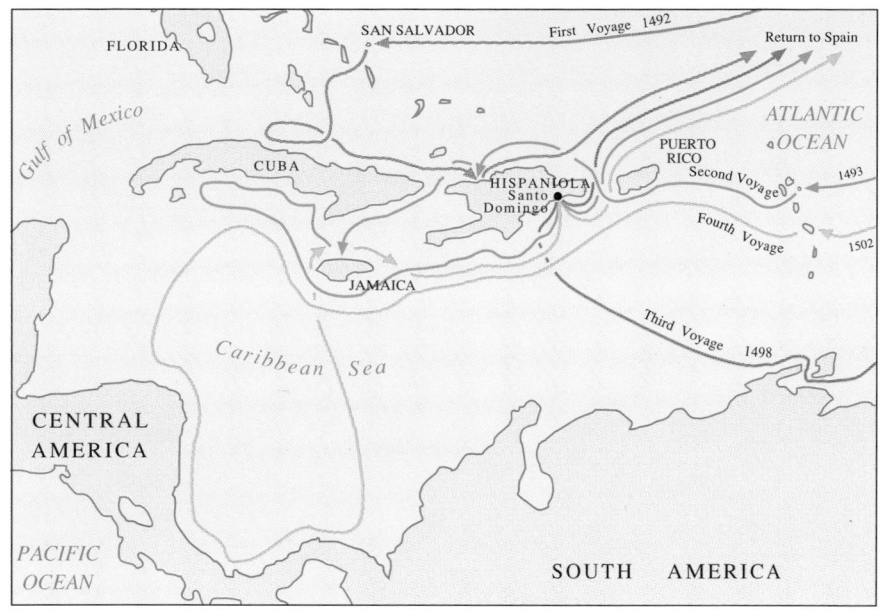

COLUMBUS'S VOYAGES TO THE NEW WORLD

fourth and final voyage in 1502, exploring the islands of the Caribbean and the coast of Central America.

Another explorer, Amerigo Vespucci, made three voyages to the Americas between 1499 and 1502. He claimed that new continents had been found. A mapmaker suggested that the new continents be named America in Vespucci's honor.

Columbian Exchange

With the arrival of Columbus in the Americas, a massive exchange of plants, animals, and diseases began between the Americas and Europe. This chart identifies some of the exchanges made.

From the Americas		To the Americas	
corn	potatoes	horses	cattle
tomatoes	chocolate	sheep	chickens
pumpkins	squashes	wheat	bananas
peppers	peanuts	sugar	grapes
pineapples	cashews	measles	smallpox

Spanish America

Conquest of the Aztecs

The Spaniards were among the leaders of the great age of European exploration. A Spaniard named Hernando Cortés sailed to Hispaniola in 1504. In 1511, he helped Diego Velázquez conquer Cuba. Then they heard about the empire of the Aztecs in what is now Mexico.

This modern painting shows Cortés and his party among the natives.

The Aztecs had formed an advanced civilization. They were a religious people, and the capital city of Tenochtitlán had many temples. The Aztecs fought many wars in the name of religion, and they sacrificed many of their prisoners to their gods. They were very wealthy, partly because they forced the tribes they conquered to surrender silver and gold.

In 1519, Cortés sailed to Mexico from Cuba and then down the coast. He and his army traveled inland to Tenochtitlán. On the way, the Spaniards were joined by many Indians

Montezuma's arrest. The Spanish soldiers in the Americas were known as conquistadores.

Spanish bring African slaves to Santo Domingo		Hernando Cortés captures Montezuma; Ferdinand Magellan begins voyage around the world	
1501	**1513**	**1519**	**1521**
	Juan Ponce de León explores Florida; Vasco Núñez de Balboa sees the Pacific Ocean		Cortés conquers the Aztecs

The Aztecs drive out Cortés and his soldiers. The Spanish returned soon and took permanent control of the empire.

who had been mistreated by the Aztecs. The Spaniards brought guns and horses, which the Indians had never seen before. In Tenochtitlán, the Spaniards captured Montezuma, the Aztec king. They forced him to pay tribute to the Spanish king.

Cortés had too few soldiers to conquer the Aztec capital, but he held Montezuma hostage to ensure the Spaniards' safety. In June 1520, the Aztecs rebelled and killed hundreds of Spaniards. However, Cortés survived. He reorganized his army and gained the support of Spanish and Indian troops. They attacked and destroyed Tenochtitlán in the spring of 1521 and built Mexico City on the ruins of the Aztec capital.

Aztec Civilization

Religion was based on hundreds of gods including a sun god, a corn god, a fire god, and a rain god. The Aztecs practiced human sacrifice.

Classes of society were nobles, commoners, serfs, and slaves. Most people were commoners who farmed or had a trade. Serfs worked the nobles' land. Slaves were criminals or people captured in war.

Aztec calendar stone

Foods were tortillas, tacos, chili peppers, corn, avocados, squash, and tomatoes.

Shelters included simple adobe homes for commoners and stone houses with patios for nobles.

Pizarro conquers the Incas

Juan Rodriguez Cabrillo explores California coast

1533 1535   **1542**   **1565**

First viceroy of New Spain is appointed

Spanish found St. Augustine, Florida

Conquest of the Incas

Like Cortés, Francisco Pizarro left Spain to explore the Americas. After living in Hispaniola, he took part in the exploration of Panama with Vasco de Balboa. Living in Panama City, Pizarro heard tales of the wealthy empire of the Incas in South America. He led several explorations down the west coast of South America to find it.

Francisco Pizarro

The Incan empire included parts of present-day Colombia, Ecuador, Peru, Bolivia, Chile, and Argentina. The Incas conquered many peoples through force and then ruled them with a complex political system. They had excellent roads and bridges. They constructed large, strong buildings of stone and made fine artwork of gold and silver. They also developed irrigation and terracing systems to improve their farming.

In 1533, Pizarro and an army of 167 troops captured the Incan leader, Atahualpa. He paid a huge ransom of gold and silver, but the Spaniards executed him anyway. The Spaniards then took over the Incan empire.

A Spanish priest teaches the Incan leader Atahualpa about Christianity. The Spanish worked to convert natives as part of their conquest of the Americas.

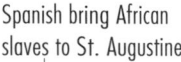
Spanish bring African slaves to St. Augustine

Spanish establish the mission and presidio of San Antonio

1581 **1609** **1718**

Spanish found the city of Santa Fe

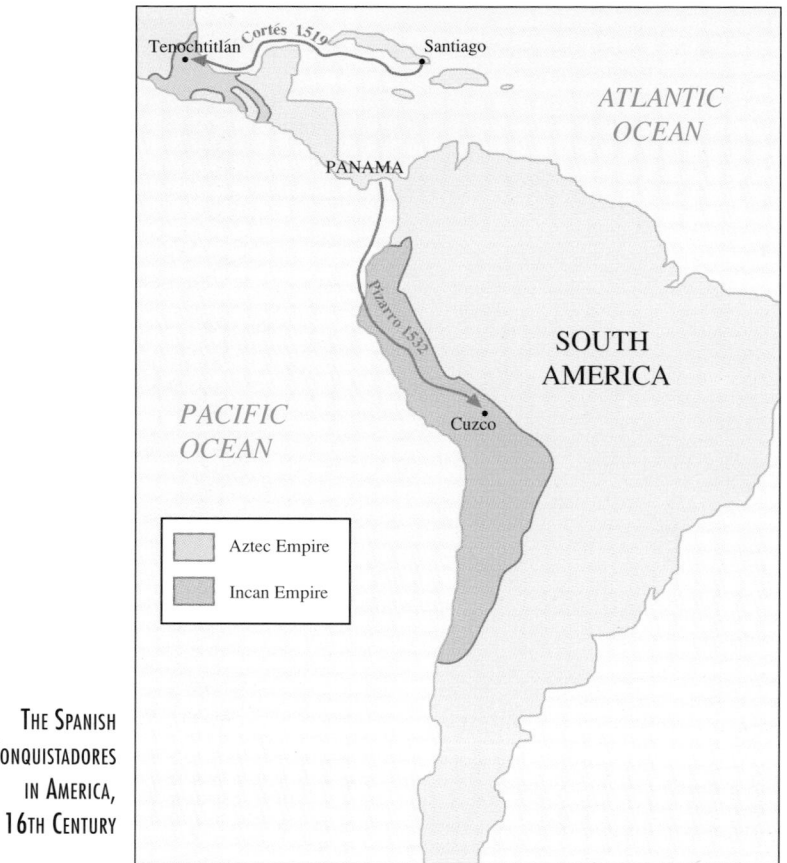

THE SPANISH CONQUISTADORES IN AMERICA, 16TH CENTURY

Incan Civilization

Religion was based on many gods, such as the creator god, the sun god, and goddesses of the earth and the sea. The Incas sacrificed crops, animals, and sometimes humans.

Classes of society were based on a family's rank. Groups called ayllus were based on family relationships and land ownership.

Foods included corn and potatoes. They also grew cotton.

Shelters included stone mansions for nobles and adobe or stone houses with thatched roofs for commoners.

Hernando de Soto and his party reach the shore of the Mississippi River.

Spanish America

In the early 1500s, Spain created the *encomienda* system in their American colonies. This meant that colonists received tracts of land and control over the Indians who lived there. The Spaniards forced the Indians to be their slaves, and many mistreated the Indians.

The Spanish did not begin exploring what is now the United States until April 1513, when Juan Ponce de León landed in Florida. De León had heard stories of a "fountain of youth," and he looked for it in present-day Florida.

The area was explored again by Hernando de Soto in 1539. He journeyed farther into the mainland and was the first European to reach the Mississippi River. Yet the area was first colonized by the French. A group of French Huguenots (a Protestant sect) settled near present-day Jacksonville in 1564. The Spanish king sent an army that founded the settlement of St. Augustine and massacred the French. St. Augustine was the first permanent European settlement in what is now the United States.

The Spanish wanted to convert the Indians to Roman Catholicism, and many priests established missions to help educate the Indians. Some also worked for better treatment of the Indians.

Between 1540 and 1542, Francisco Vasquez de Coronado went in search of the legendary seven cities of great wealth. He ended up in what is now New Mexico and Arizona. Other Spanish explorers traveled through the region and finally colonized it in 1598.

The Spanish Influence in America

The Palace of the Governors today.

Did you know that you can visit a building constructed by the Spanish in America in 1609? The Spanish built the Palace of the Governors in Santa Fe, New Mexico, in 1609 as a fortress. The Spanish builders used adobe, a kind of sun-dried brick. Although the builders used American materials, the architectural style is mainly Spanish, with a covered porch and European-style doors and windows.

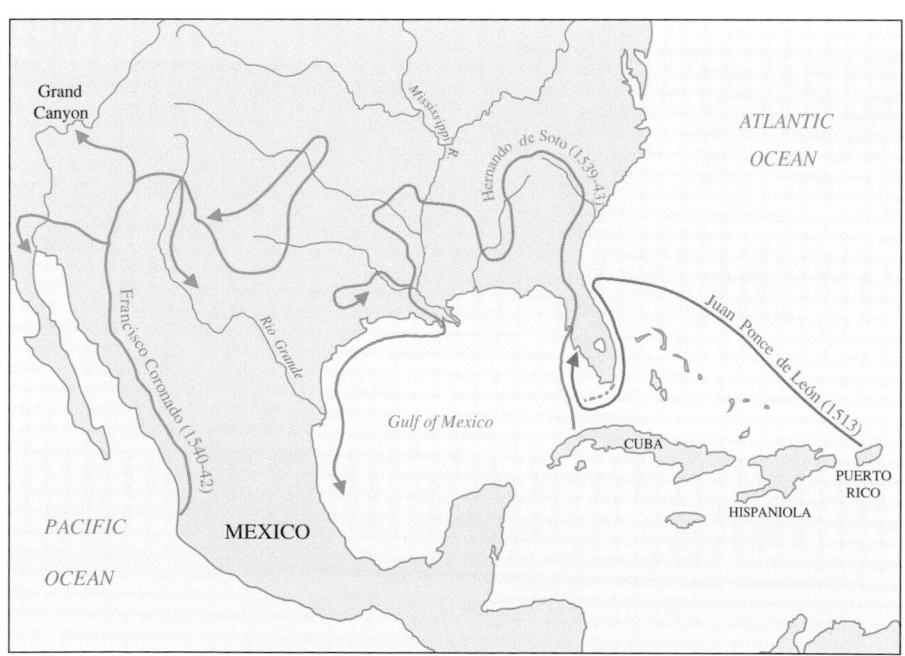

SPANISH EXPLORERS IN NORTH AMERICA, 16TH CENTURY

French and English Exploration

In Search of the Northwest Passage

After Columbus's voyages, the French and English continued to look for a shorter route to the Far East. In looking for a Northwest Passage through North America, explorers from these two countries searched much of the coast of North America. In 1524, Giovanni da Verrazano commanded a French voyage to look for the Northwest Passage. Verrazano explored the Atlantic coast and reported on its beauty to the king of France.

Giovanni da Verrazano

Searching for gold and for a Northwest Passage, Jacques Cartier of France sailed up the St. Lawrence River in 1534 to the site of present-day Montreal. English explorer Henry Hudson, sailing for the Netherlands, also explored Canada. He sailed into what is now known as Hudson

Jacques Cartier

Giovanni da Verrazano explores the eastern coast of North America

English bring African slaves to Hispaniola

English defeat the Spanish Armada

| 1524 | 1534 | 1565 | 1587 | 1588 |

Jacques Cartier sails into the Gulf of St. Lawrence

English set up their first North American settlement on Roanoke Island

Hudson did not find a northern route to the Indies, but he did leave a mark on North America. Hudson Bay, Hudson Strait, and the Hudson River all bear his name.

Bay, believing he had found the Pacific Ocean. His ship was trapped by ice. After a harsh winter, his crew left Hudson and returned to England. Hudson's fate is unknown, but his explorations led to later claims and settlement by the Dutch.

In 1584, Sir Walter Raleigh of England sent explorers to the North American coast to find a good place for a colony. They chose Roanoke Island in North Carolina and started a settlement there in 1587. John White, the settlement's governor, returned to England. When he came back to Roanoke in 1590, the colony had mysteriously disappeared. Search parties found only the word *Croatoan* carved in a tree. The Croatoans were Indians who had been friendly with the settlers. Some people thought that the settlers had moved north to the Chesapeake Bay area and fought with Indians there. Others thought that the settlers scattered and ended up living with several different Indian tribes. No one knows for sure what happened to the settlers, so the group is known as the **Lost Colony.**

1606	1608	1610	1642	1667	1673

Samuel de Champlain founds Quebec (1608)

French establish Montreal (1642)

Louis Joliet and Jacques Marquette explore the Mississippi River (1673)

English set up companies to colonize America (1606)

Henry Hudson explores Hudson Bay (1610)

French sign a peace treaty with Iroquois (1667)

Fur traders were some of the first Europeans to successfully settle in North America.

The French in Canada

After Jacques Cartier explored the land around the St. Lawrence River, French fishing crews and traders began to settle in the area. The traders exchanged European goods such as tools and knives with the Indians for furs from beavers, foxes, minks, and otters. Europeans used the furs to make hats and other clothing; hats made from beaver fur became especially popular. By the late 1500s, the fur trade had become an important industry.

In 1608, the French explorer Samuel de Champlain founded the town of Quebec on the St. Lawrence River. Quebec

Champlain selects the site of Quebec.

became an important fur trading center and the center of culture in the growing colony of New France. New France included Canada, Acadia, and Louisiana. In 1660, the colony consisted of only a few thousand fur traders and missionaries. In 1663, King Louis XIV of France sent 2,500 new settlers. By 1720, New France's population was 25,000.

The fur trade remained the most important industry in New France. However, farming also developed. Many young fur traders became farmers when they married. They rented sections of land called *seigneuries*. The king of France gave these parcels of farmland to colonists who had been wealthy nobles or military officers in France.

The colony of New France thrived for 150 years. The Catholic church ran schools and hospitals. The wealthy leaders of the colony lived in large, luxurious houses and enjoyed social events such as formal balls. Merchants lived in smaller stone houses, and farmers lived in small log cabins.

The French colony of Quebec as it looked in 1775.

English Colonies

Natives welcome the English settlers as they land on the shores of Virginia.

Jamestown

On May 6, 1607, a group of 105 English adventurers landed on a peninsula on the James River in what is now Virginia. The colonists had been sent to start a settlement by a business called the Virginia Company of London. They called their settlement Jamestown in honor of their king, James I.

The settlers chose a swampy, unhealthy site for their home. They had poor diets, and two thirds of them died of malnutrition or of diseases such as malaria and pneumonia. In 1608, Captain John Smith took control of the colony. Smith made the settlers plant food crops. He also bought corn from Indians. After Smith returned to England in 1609, Lord De La Warr brought new settlers and supplies in 1610.

The Jamestown settlers worried about problems with the Indians. Pocahontas, the daughter of the leader of the Virginia Indian tribes, helped keep peace for a time. She married set-

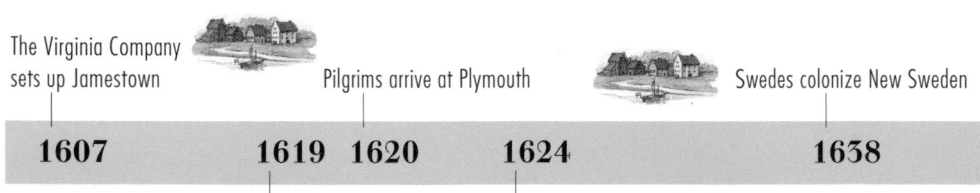

The Virginia Company sets up Jamestown

Pilgrims arrive at Plymouth

Swedes colonize New Sweden

1607   **1619** **1620**   **1624**   **1638**

House of Burgesses is formed

Dutch settlers begin New Netherland colony

Pocahontas, daughter of the powerful chief Powhatan, asks that John Smith's life be spared to keep peace during a dispute between the Indians and the Jamestown colonists.

The first Jamestown settlers work to build their colony.

tler John Rolfe, who introduced a new tobacco plant that became a valuable cash crop. Soon, the colony raised hogs as well and grew plenty of corn.

In 1619, the Virginia Company sent some young women to Jamestown. They married colonists and began families. Indians fearing the loss of their homes attacked the settlement in 1622 and 1644. Fires destroyed the town in 1676 and 1698. Still, Jamestown paved the way for more English colonies.

The House of Burgesses

In 1619, the governor of Virginia called a meeting to be attended by two citizens from each of the divisions of Virginia. At that time, only adult males were considered citizens. These citizen representatives were called burgesses. The **House of Burgesses** first met on July 30, 1619, in Jamestown. The House of Burgesses followed English law, acted on all tax laws, and made other laws. After 1625, the house began managing all of the colony's affairs. The House of Burgesses was an important step in American democracy.

English establish the Carolinas

New Englanders win Prince Philip's War against the Indians

1651	1663	1664	1676	1732

English Parliament passes the first Navigation Act

English take over New Netherland and New Sweden

James Oglethorpe founds Georgia

The first colonists from the *Mayflower* arrive at Plymouth.

Plymouth

The people who later became known as the **Pilgrims** of Plymouth Colony left England because they wanted religious freedom. The official English church was the Church of England. People who did not belong to this religion were often persecuted. The Pilgrims had separated from the Church of England and began practicing religion in their own way. Some fled to the Netherlands, but they were unhappy that their children were not living as English citizens.

Because they wished to worship in their own way in an English environment, the Pilgrims decided to leave for America. Here they believed that they could practice their religion and live under English ways of life. The Pilgrims sailed on the *Mayflower* for over two months and landed on Cape Cod on November 20, 1620. Although they meant to land farther south near Virginia, the settlers arrived in New England because of navigational errors and bad weather.

While still aboard the *Mayflower*, 41 settlers signed the **Mayflower Compact**. Because they were settling outside the area granted to them, the Pilgrims did not have a set of

The signing of the Mayflower Compact.

rules by which to live. The Mayflower Compact set up a few basic rules that all Plymouth settlers had to follow. It was the first guide to self-government created in the American colonies. The Mayflower Compact set up a General Court, which was in charge of electing leaders, imposing taxes, and making laws.

Harvest Festival

After founding the Plymouth Colony in 1620, the Pilgrims suffered through a long, harsh winter. They did not know how to produce the food they needed until their Indian friend Squanto showed them American crops and farming methods. When

they harvested a bountiful crop in the autumn of 1621, they invited the Indians to join them in a three-day harvest celebration. They enjoyed American foods such as cornbread, duck, goose, turkey, venison (deer meat), and shellfish.

The Narraganset Indians grant land to Roger Williams, who had always encouraged peaceful, humane relations with the Indians.

Massachusetts, Rhode Island, Connecticut, and Maryland

In 1630, a group called the **Puritans** came to the Massachusetts Bay area in search of religious freedom. By 1640, the Massachusetts Bay Colony had 10,000 people. The Puritans favored political freedom that gave people certain basic rights. However, only people who practiced the Puritan religion were allowed to live in the colony.

Many settlers left Massachusetts because of the strict religious rules. Some, like Roger Williams, were driven out. In 1636, he bought land from the Narraganset Indians and established the town of Providence, Rhode Island. He set up a government based on religious and political freedom. Other settlers from Massachusetts set up the towns of Portsmouth, Newport, and Warwick.

The Maryland colonists established friendly ties with the Indians in the region.

Colonists from Massachusetts also settled Connecticut. Thomas Hooker, a minister, came searching for religious and political freedom. Others came in search of good farmland. The colonists founded several settlements, and in 1636, they were united as the Connecticut Colony.

In 1634, a group of English colonists settled in Maryland. The owner of the colony's charter in England was Lord Baltimore. Lord Baltimore was a Roman Catholic. He felt that religious freedom would encourage the growth of the Maryland colony. Maryland soon allowed the practice of all Christian religions.

Lord Baltimore

The Road to Democracy

Many of the first English settlers in America insisted on religious freedom. Their search for religious freedom often led them to establish political self-government. In Connecticut, Thomas Hooker's call for a government by the people led to the **Fundamental Orders**. The Orders provided for government elections by citizens. The Puritans of Massachusetts created a similar document, the **Body of Liberties**, in 1641. Massachusetts set up a system that allowed citizens—males who owned property—enforce their own laws. In Maryland, Lord Baltimore's insistence on religious freedom for all Christians led to the **Toleration Act of 1649**.

Thomas Hooker and his settlers arrive at Hartford, Connecticut.

New Netherland and New Sweden

Dutch settler Peter Minuit negotiates for the island of Manhattan. The Indians offered rights for the land and accepted a variety of goods worth about 60 guilders, or 24 dollars.

Merchants in the Netherlands wanted to compete with the French and Spanish in the American fur trade. In 1621, they formed the Dutch West India Company. In 1624, the company sent colonists to settle near the mouth of the Hudson River on an island that the Indians called Man-a-hat-ta. The Dutch colonists called their settlement New Amsterdam. In 1626, the governor of the settlement, Peter Minuit, bought the island of Manhattan from the Indians.

The Dutch claimed land including parts of present-day Connecticut, Delaware, New Jersey, and New York. In order to colonize their land quickly, they set up the **patroon system**. Huge pieces of land were given to patroons (landowners), who were to find 50 adults to settle on the land and farm it. However, the strict patroons gave their workers few rights, so the population grew slowly.

Dutch governor Peter Stuyvesant recaptured Fort Casimir from the Swedish on September 26, 1655. This victory ended a 15-year struggle between Dutch and Swedish colonists by driving the Swedes out of North America.

In 1638, Swedish settlers founded a colony in present-day New Jersey. The Dutch, who lived directly north of New Sweden, believed that the Swedes were on Dutch land. The Swedish colony numbered fewer than 200 people. The Dutch governor, Peter Stuyvesant, took over the Swedish colony in 1655.

Many English colonists from Massachusetts and Connecticut settled eastern Long Island off the coast of New Amsterdam. The Dutch settled on the western part. The Dutch and the English lived in peace for several years, but then they began to fight. The king of England gave his brother, the Duke of York, a charter for the territory. In 1664, English warships sailed into the New Amsterdam harbor. The Dutch colonists would not support Peter Stuyvesant, and they surrendered the colony. The English renamed the area New York after the Duke of York.

Stuyvesant surrendered New Amsterdam to Colonel Richard Nicolls on September 20, 1664, almost nine years to the day after ousting the Swedish colonists.

William Penn establishes a treaty with neighboring Indians. Fair treatment of natives was an important part of Penn's plan for his colony.

Pennsylvania, Carolinas, and Georgia

In 1663, the king of England granted present-day North Carolina and South Carolina to **proprietors**, or owners. They named the land Carolina after their king, Charles II. Beginning in 1670, the proprietors sent colonists to the land and accepted others who came as well. By 1700, the colony contained many wealthy plantations worked by slaves, who made up about half the population.

Meanwhile, North Carolina was being settled by people from Virginia and England. The proprietors allowed the colonists to govern themselves. Most lived on small farms and had fewer slaves than their neighbors to the south.

In 1681, the king of England granted the Pennsylvania region to William Penn. Penn was a **Quaker**, a believer in a new faith based on peace and goodwill. He planned to establish

King Charles II presents the charter for Pennsylvania to William Penn as payment of a debt owed to Penn's father.

James Oglethorpe

a colony with political and religious freedom. Penn laid out the plan for the capital city of Philadelphia in 1682. Both the city and the colony prospered.

James Oglethorpe wanted to help the jailed debtors of England start a new life, so he and some wealthy friends sent them to settle Georgia. At first, the colonists were granted only small parcels of land and were not allowed slaves. Georgia later developed a plantation economy.

Penn's Dream

William Penn was a Quaker. The Quakers believed that religious authority came from the Christian spirit in each person, not from the Bible or priests. They thought that killing was wrong, even in war. William Penn wanted to create a colony where Quakers could worship freely. He soon decided to make his colony a refuge for any people who wanted religious or political liberty.

William Penn

On the colonial plantations in the South, life was very different for the slaves (*left*) than it was for the landowners (*below*).

Colonial Economies

Settlers soon learned how to live off of America's rich resources. Farming became the most important way of life. Most farmers planted the same crop for several years. When the soil ran out of nutrients, the farmers cleared more land. Since the East Coast had plenty of rich soil, farmers produced plenty of food. In addition to growing corn and wheat, they raised livestock. Farmers in Virginia and Maryland grew tobacco. Those in Georgia and South Carolina produced rice and indigo. Another valuable product was timber. Lumber and other tree products were important for the shipbuilding industry.

In the South, African slaves did most of the hard work on tobacco, rice, and indigo **plantations.** By 1750, more than 235,000 African slaves lived in the colonies.

Shipbuilding, whaling, and fishing were all important industries in the colonies.

The farming in New England was more difficult than in the other colonies. The climate was harsher, the land was rockier, and the soil was thinner. Many people turned to fishing and whaling. The nearness of the sea also encouraged the ship-building industry in New England.

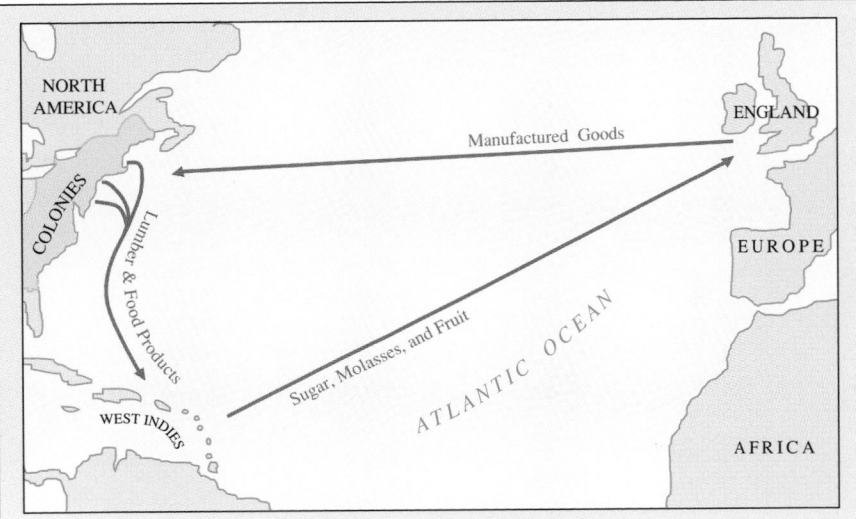

TRIANGULAR TRADE ROUTE, 18TH CENTURY

Trade with the English

When Americans began to produce enough goods for export to other places, England made laws called the **Navigation Acts.** The acts forced the colonies to trade only with England and regulated what could be exported. One of the acts, the Molasses Act, prohibited the colonies from buying molasses from the French colonies in the West Indies. However, the colonists smuggled in French molasses. To get around other navigation laws, the colonies developed **triangular trade routes.** One of these routes involved sending food products and lumber to the West Indies. The West Indies exchanged these products for fruit, molasses, and sugar. These were traded to England for manufactured goods, which were exported to the colonies.

Life in the Colonies

The **New England Colonies** included Massachusetts, Rhode Island, Connecticut, and New Hampshire. New England life centered around towns. Settlers were given a piece of land for a house, a lot on which to plant corn, and part of a common meadow on which their animals could graze. Decisions about the towns were made in town meetings. Salem and Boston, two towns in Massachusetts, were the main trade ports in New England.

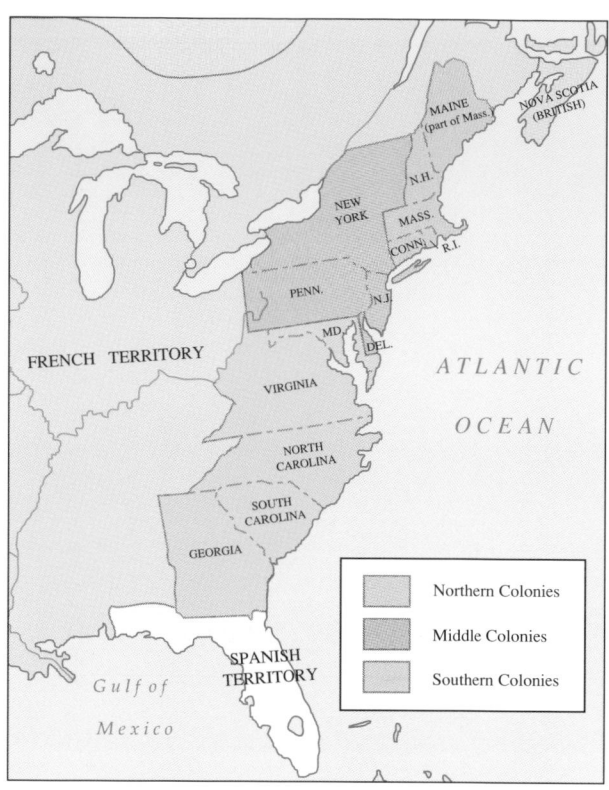

THE ENGLISH COLONIES IN AMERICA, 18TH CENTURY

The **Middle Colonies** included Delaware, New Jersey, New York, and Pennsylvania. Many farmers produced so much wheat that the colonies became known as the "bread colonies." The Middle Colonies also manufactured glass and leather goods. The two largest American cities, Philadelphia and New York, were located here.

The **Southern Colonies** included Georgia, Maryland, North Carolina, South Carolina, and Virginia. This is where life on the big tobacco and indigo plantations thrived. Slaves

A typical street in the colony of New York might have looked like this on a given day.

The city of Yorktown, Virginia, as it appeared in 1781.

were the main workers on the plantations, and they made up a large part of the population in the South. Charleston, South Carolina, and Savannah, Georgia, were two of the main port cities where slaves and goods were traded.

The Great Awakening

In colonial times, many people lived far from a church. During the **Great Awakening**, from the mid-1740s until about 1750, several popular ministers traveled throughout the colonies and held huge meetings. These preachers spoke about repenting sins and turning to God. One result of these revivals was that new Methodist and Baptist congregations sprang up. Also, the preachers helped the colonists think about the equality of all people. Finally, the Great Awakening improved higher education. In order to educate new preachers, church leaders founded the College of New Jersey at Princeton in 1746, King's College (Columbia University) in 1754, the College of Rhode Island (later Brown University) in 1764, and Queen's College (Rutgers University) in 1766.

George Whitfield was an influential traveling preacher.

Jonathan Edwards helped inspire the Great Awakening.

Colonial Strife

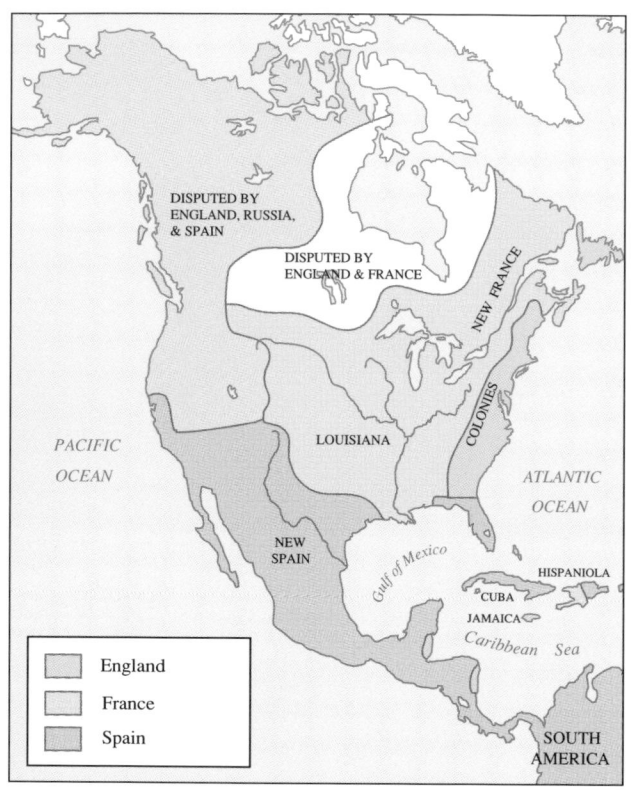

EUROPEAN CLAIMS IN NORTH AMERICA, 1748

The French and Indian War

The French owned land along the St. Lawrence River, the Great Lakes, and the Mississippi River. England claimed the land lying inland from its colonies. The two countries fought over their lands and over control of the fur-trading and fishing industries in America.

The French and Indian War began in 1754. The French had many friends among the Indian tribes. The English had often cheated and killed their Indian neighbors. Many Indians helped the French fight the English.

The French had several successes in 1755 and 1756. A strong general, the Marquis de Montcalm, led the French in capturing

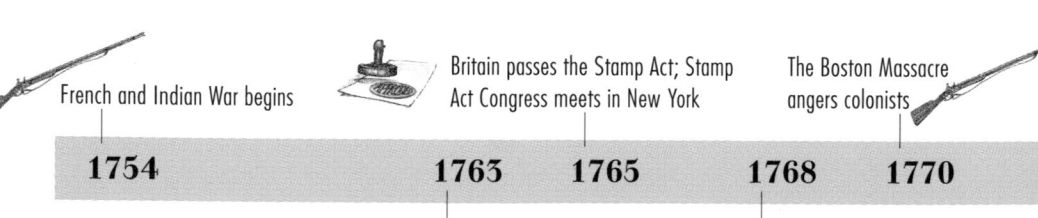

French and Indian War begins

Britain passes the Stamp Act; Stamp Act Congress meets in New York

The Boston Massacre angers colonists

1754   **1763**   **1765**   **1768**   **1770**

Treaty of Paris signed; Britain enforces Navigation Acts in the colonies

The British send soldiers to Boston to keep order

In an early victory, English forces at Lake George stop the French from invading New York.

British strongholds. From 1758 to 1759, the British defeated the French at important forts along the western frontier. Finally, the British captured Quebec in 1759 and Montreal in 1760.

The French and Indian War was part of the Seven Years' War waged by the major European nations. To end the war, the **Treaty of Paris** in 1763 gave Britain almost all the French lands in Canada and east of the Mississippi River. Spain received New Orleans and French lands west of the Mississippi. The war put an end to France's strength in North America.

DISPUTED BY ENGLAND, RUSSIA, & SPAIN

PACIFIC OCEAN

LOUISIANA

COLONIES

ATLANTIC OCEAN

NEW SPAIN

Gulf of Mexico

HISPANIOLA

CUBA

JAMAICA

Caribbean Sea

SOUTH AMERICA

- England
- France
- Spain

EUROPEAN CLAIMS IN NORTH AMERICA, 1763

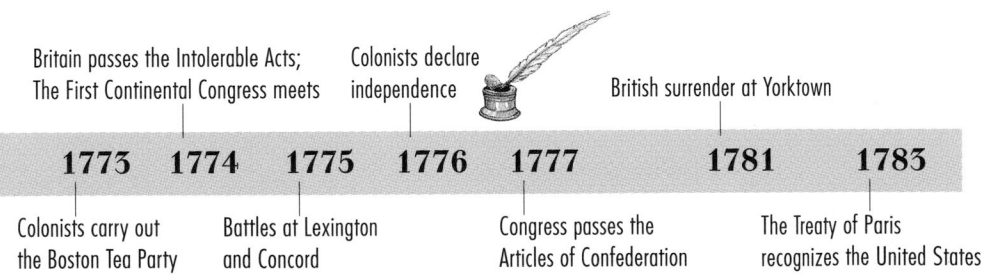

Britain passes the Intolerable Acts; The First Continental Congress meets

Colonists declare independence

British surrender at Yorktown

1773   1774   1775   1776   1777   1781   1783

Colonists carry out the Boston Tea Party

Battles at Lexington and Concord

Congress passes the Articles of Confederation

The Treaty of Paris recognizes the United States

After the Boston Massacre, British troops were moved out of the city to ease tensions. A trial found two of the soldiers involved in the incident guilty of manslaughter.

Stamp Act Congress

After the French and Indian War, Britain had a much greater territory to control in America. Also, the expensive war had greatly increased Britain's national debt. The British Parliament felt that the colonies should help pay for these expenses. To get additional revenue from the colonies, Britain began to exert a tighter rule over the American colonies, which upset many colonists.

The Stamp Act of 1765 required colonists to buy stamps for paper documents, such as newspapers, pamphlets, and legal documents. Many colonists argued that since America was not represented in Parliament, Parliament did not have the right to tax them. Some

Americans throughout the colonies violently protested the Stamp Act.

colonists organized a group called the **Sons of Liberty**. They encouraged colonists not to obey the Stamp Act and not to import British goods.

In October 1765, representatives from nine colonies met in New York to discuss the Stamp Act. This was known as the Stamp Act Congress. The colonists agreed that "taxation without representation is tyranny." Parliament soon repealed the Stamp Act.

In 1767, Parliament passed the **Townshend Acts**, which taxed such British imports as paint, lead, paper, and tea. The British sent troops to New York and Boston to put down protests. The Bostonians especially objected to their presence. On March 5, 1770, an unruly American mob attacked some British soldiers. The soldiers fired on the crowd and killed four Boston citizens. This was known as the **Boston Massacre**.

That same day, Parliament repealed all of the Townshend duties except for the tax on tea. This the British kept to assert their authority over the colonists.

Important Acts and People

Sugar Act was passed to raise revenue. It restricted American exports and put additional taxes on some imports.

Stamp Act of 1765 required American businesses to buy stamps for many kinds of documents.

Townshend Acts of 1767 required Americans to pay taxes on imports of lead, paint, paper, and tea.

John Dickinson published the "Pennsylvania Farmer" letters to convince people to settle the disagreements between Britain and the colonies peacefully.

Patrick Henry led the opposition to the Stamp Act in Virginia.

Samuel Adams helped organize the Sons of Liberty and publicized the unfairness of the Townshend Acts.

Crispus Attucks, an African American and a former slave, became one of the first to give his life in the Revolution when he was killed at the Boston Massacre.

Colonists disguised as Mohawk Indians dump tea from the *Dartmouth* into Boston Harbor.

The Beginning of War

With the new taxes and laws, some Americans feared that the British would soon take away all their freedom. In 1773, Parliament gave the East India Company a monopoly on all tea sent to the colonies. The colonies reacted angrily. In Philadelphia and New York, the tea was returned to England.

In Charleston, the tea was allowed to land but was not sold. In Boston, the Sons of Liberty dumped the tea into the water. This **Boston Tea Party** angered Parliament, and in 1774, England passed several laws to punish the colonies. The Americans called these laws the **Intolerable Acts**.

Patrick Henry

In response to the Intolerable Acts, the colonies planned a congress of all the American colonies. On May 27, 1774, delegates from all the colonies except Georgia met in Philadelphia. This was the **First Continental Congress**. The Congress called for an end to trade with Britain until the Intolerable

Two famous incidents from the beginning of the Revolutionary War: Paul Revere's ride *(left)* and the Battle of Lexington *(below).*

Acts were repealed. It declared that Parliament had no right to pass laws for America except those involving foreign trade. Some of the leaders at the Congress were Richard Henry Lee, Patrick Henry, George Washington, and John Jay.

King George III insisted that the colonies would not become independent without a fight. On April 19, 1775, British troops were sent to seize American ammunition at Concord, outside Boston. Two American patriots, William Dawes and Paul Revere, rode through the countryside to warn the citizens, and the **Minutemen**, armed colonists, were waiting at Lexington for the soldiers. Shots rang out, and the Revolutionary War had begun.

Revolutionary War

	Americans	British
Advantages	•On American land •Leadership of George Washington •Help from France	•Strong government •Trained army •Financial resources
Disadvantages	•Lack of finances •Untrained army •Weak government	•Lack of enthusiasm •Far from home •American sympathizers in Britain

The Declaration of Independence

The Continental Congress signed the Declaration of Independence on July 4, 1776.

Even after Lexington and Concord, Americans disagreed over whether or not they should be independent from Great Britain. In 1775, the Continental Congress sent the **Olive Branch Petition** to King George III. The petition promised loyalty to the king and asked for compromise. King George did not trust the Americans. He declared that the colonies were in a state of rebellion. In January 1776, **Thomas Paine** published a pamphlet called *Common Sense*. It said that Americans must become independent. Paine's words helped change people's minds. In 1776, the Congress passed the Declaration of Independence. Written by **Thomas Jefferson,** the Declaration laid out some basic ideas on which a government should be based. It also gave the reasons why America should become independent.

Loyalists and Patriots

Some people in the colonies remained loyal to England. These **Loyalists** made up about one third of the American population. Many were leaders of the government, church, or military. They feared that they would lose their positions if they opposed England. They also respected the King of England's authority. Many Loyalists left America at the beginning of the war. Others stayed in the colonies. The **Patriots** were Americans who supported war against Britain.

The Revolution

When fighting against the British started, each colony had its own militia. **George Washington,** the general in command of the war, organized the Continental Army, but he had a difficult time recruiting soldiers. One of the colonies' greatest strengths was General George Washington.

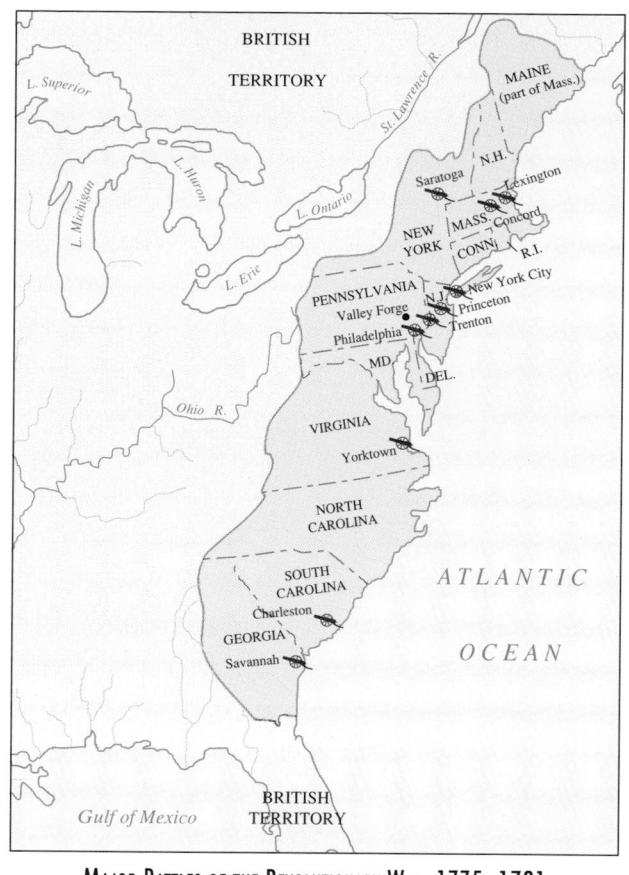

MAJOR BATTLES OF THE REVOLUTIONARY WAR, 1775–1781

The British had a strong army, and they hired German mercenaries (paid soldiers). Britain planned to defeat the colonies in the north first. They hoped that the other colonies would then surrender. The British captured New York City in 1776. Washington countered with a surprise attack on Trenton, New Jersey. The Americans also defeated the British at Princeton, New Jersey.

The British captured Philadelphia on September 26, 1777. Benedict Arnold led battles against British General John Burgoyne near Saratoga, New York. On October 17, 1777, Burgoyne surrendered. This was a turning point of the war, because France then agreed to help the Americans.

Washington's army endured a terrible winter at Valley Forge, Pennsylvania. While they were there, a Prussian soldier named Baron Friedrich von Steuben taught them military methods. By the end of 1778, the British brought forces into

On Christmas day 1776, George Washington led colonial troops across the Delaware River for a successful surprise attack on Trenton, New Jersey.

the Southern Colonies. They captured Savannah, Georgia, and later took Charleston, South Carolina.

Yorktown, Virginia, was the site of the last major battle. French and Americans surrounded British troops led by General Cornwallis. Cornwallis surrendered on October 19, 1781. The Americans and the British signed the **Treaty of Paris** in 1783.

Some Heroes of the Revolution

Mary Hayes accompanied her husband at the Battle of Monmouth and earned the nickname "Molly Pitcher" for bringing water to soldiers.

John Paul Jones was a naval captain who captured the British ship *Serapis* in 1779. In the midst of battle, Jones said, "I have not yet begun to fight."

Marquis de Lafayette was a French noble who led troops in the Battle of Yorktown.

Francis Marion, known as the "Swamp Fox" for his guerrilla attacks, helped force Cornwallis to Yorktown.

Casimir Pulaski, a professional soldier from Poland, died in battle at Savannah.

A New Nation

The Articles of Confederation

In 1777, Congress passed the Articles of Confederation. These articles gave the national government the power to declare war and deal with other countries. But the government could not collect taxes. It had no way to pay back the huge debts from the war or to provide for an army. The states limited the power of the national government so that each state would have more control over its own affairs.

UNITED STATES TERRITORY IN 1781

Articles of Confederation

National Congress Could:
•Declare war and peace
•Manage foreign relations
•Establish army and navy
•Issue and borrow money
•Control Indian affairs

Each State Government Could:
•Have one vote in Congress
•Have any powers not specifically given to the Congress

Weaknesses:
•Congress could not raise money through taxes or control trade
•Congress could not enforce its laws on the states
•No federal executive or judiciary branch

The Constitutional Convention

In 1786, farmers in Massachusetts were deep in debt. Their state taxes were very high, and prices for farm products were low. Groups of farmers demanded financial help. The state government refused their demands. Daniel Shays, a Revolutionary War veteran, led a group of 1,200 farmers to take over the Springfield arsenal. They were turned back and arrested. Shays and others were later pardoned. **Shays' Rebellion** helped people realize that the federal government needed more control over finances.

Economic problems in Massachusetts in the 1780s led to violent conflicts between citizens and the government.

In 1787, fifty-five delegates, from all states except Rhode Island, met for the Constitutional Convention and set up an entirely new government. The first plan proposed was the Virginia Plan. Many delegates,

George Washington addresses the Constitutional Convention.

Congress approves the Articles of Confederation

Articles are ratified by all states

Congress passes a Land Ordinance

1777   **1780** **1781**   **1783**   **1785**   **1787**

Pennsylvania becomes the first state to ban slavery

Treaty of Paris is signed

Congress passes the Northwest Ordinance; Constitutional Convention assembles

especially those from small states, opposed the plan because it based the number of representatives on a state's population. Some offered the New Jersey Plan. It was much like the Articles of Confederation, but with a stronger Congress. The **Great Compromise** settled the argument. It proposed two houses of Congress with membership in the lower house based on a state's population. In the other house, each state would have the same number of representatives.

The members also disagreed over how to choose an executive, or President. This time, the compromise proposed that an **electoral college** would choose the executive. All 13 states ratified the Constitution by May 1790.

Creators of the Constitution

Benjamin Franklin

The oldest delegate was **Benjamin Franklin**, who was 81 and in poor health.

Alexander Hamilton fought for a strong federal government.

James Madison was called the "Father of the Constitution."

Gouverneur Morris wrote the final revision of the Constitution.

Edmund Randolph proposed the Virginia Plan.

Roger Sherman suggested the Great Compromise.

George Washington was president of the convention.

The Constitution is ratified; the Bill of Rights is proposed

Bill of Rights is ratified

Washington signs Jay's Treaty with England

1788   1789   1791   1793   1795   1796

George Washington elected President

Washington is sworn in for a second term as President

John Adams elected President

The Constitution

The Constitution

The Constitution allows United States citizens to elect the people who will represent them in government. It also sets up a **federal** system. This means that powers are divided between the national and the state governments. In the national government, power is divided among three branches. The **executive branch,** the President, enforces the law. The **legislative branch,** the Congress, makes the law. The **judicial branch,** the Supreme Court, explains the law.

Articles I, II, and III describe the branches of the government. These articles explain how the President, Vice-president, senators, representatives, and Supreme Court justices are chosen. It describes the powers and responsibilities of each office. The federal powers listed include the right to collect taxes, to declare war, and to regulate trade. These are called expressed powers. The Constitution also includes some reserved powers. These are powers, such as marriage and public education, that are not given to the federal government and, therefore, belong to the people or to the states.

Article IV says that all states are equal to one another and that new states may be admitted to the Union. Article V explains how **amendments** may be added to the Constitution. Article VI says that when state laws conflict with national laws, the national laws come first. It also says that a national law must not contradict the Constitution. Article VII explains that the Constitution had to be ratified by at least nine states to become law.

Checks and Balances

The U.S. Constitution provides a system of checks and balances in the government. Each of the three branches of the government has powers that let them influence what the other branches do. This way, all three branches

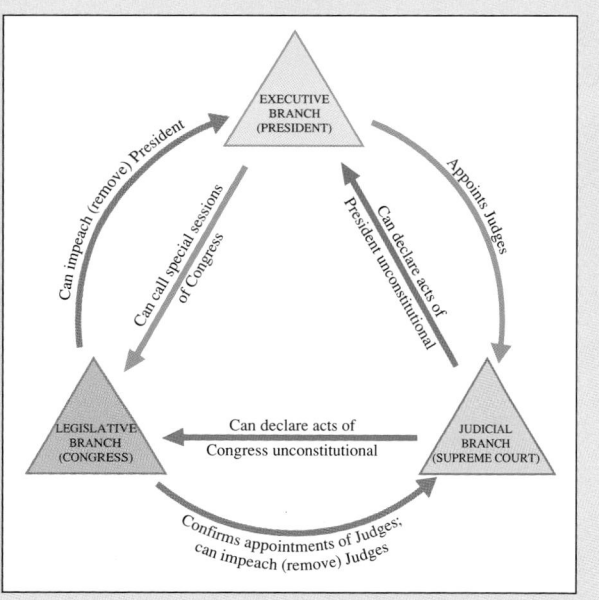

must work together to run the country, and no one branch can become so powerful that it takes control of the country.

A New Nation: The Bill of Rights

The United States Constitution focused on creating a strong government. It did not discuss the basic rights of all citizens. Some states would not ratify the Constitution unless a Bill of Rights was added. The Bill of Rights was ratified on December 15, 1791 and guarantees the following freedoms:

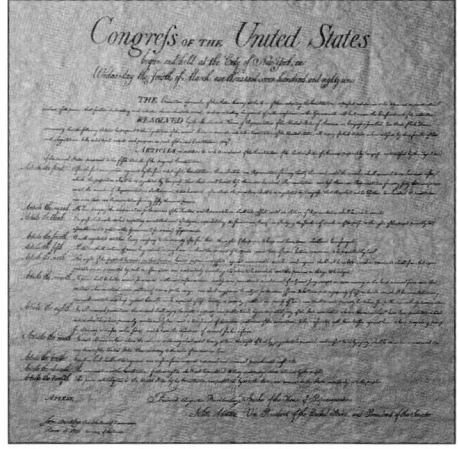

The Bill of Rights

Amendment 1: Freedom of religion, speech, and the press; rights of assembly and petition.

Amendment 2: Right to bear arms.

Amendment 3: No citizen will be required to house soldiers.

Amendment 4: Authorities must have an arrest or search warrant before arresting people or searching their homes.

Amendment 5: Rights in criminal cases.

Amendment 6: Rights to a fair trial.

Amendment 7: Rights in civil cases.

Amendment 8: Bails, fines, and punishments must be fair.

Amendment 9: People have other rights not listed in the Constitution.

Amendment 10: Powers not given to the federal government are reserved for the states or the people.

The founders of the Constitution thought that the Constitution should be flexible. They provided for a way to add amendments, or changes. Two thirds of each house of Congress must pass an amendment. Or Congress may set up a national convention to pass it. Then the legislatures of three fourths of the states must ratify it.

How a Bill Becomes a Law

A bill, or proposed law, can be introduced in either the House of Representatives or the Senate, unless it is a money bill. Only the House of Representatives can propose money bills.

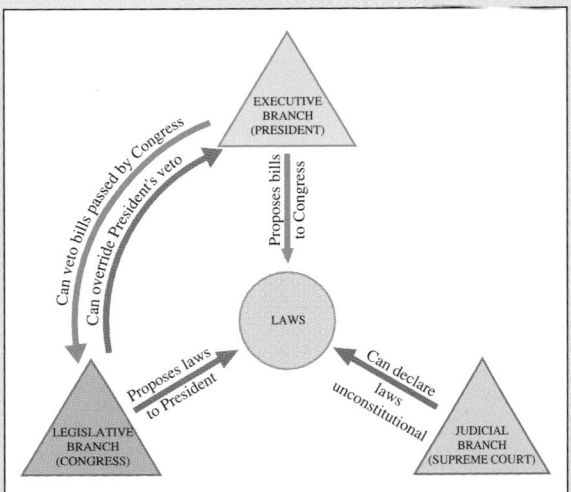

1. A bill is introduced to one of the houses of Congress and assigned a number.

2. A committee collects information about the bill, holds hearings, and suggests changes. Then it is presented to the entire house.

3. The house discusses the bill and then votes on it. If approved by more than half the members, it is sent to the other house.

4. The bill goes through the same process in the other house.

5. The bill goes to a conference committee made up of members of both houses. The conference committee revises it if necessary.

6. Both houses vote on the revised bill. If approved, it is sent to the President.

7. If the President signs it, the bill becomes law.

8. If the President vetoes the bill, the Congress can override the veto. This means that the bill will become law if two thirds of both houses approve it over the President's veto.

George Washington was sworn in as President on April 30, 1789, in New York City.

President Washington

The electoral college unanimously elected George Washington the first President of the United States in 1789. For his **Cabinet,** he appointed **Thomas Jefferson** Secretary of State; **Alexander Hamilton** Secretary of the Treasury; **Henry Knox** Secretary of War; and **Edmund Randolph** Attorney General.

Alexander Hamilton wanted to increase tariffs and to tax some products. This money would be used to pay national and state debts. Jefferson did not like the plan, but he agreed to support it in exchange for Hamilton's support of a new capital city on the Potomac River.

One result of Hamilton's tax policies was the **Whiskey Rebellion.** In 1794, liquor producers in Pennsylvania refused to pay the liquor tax. Washington sent in troops to end the rebellion. This showed how national laws could be enforced.

Pennsylvania liquor producers tar and feather a tax collector to protest taxes imposed by the national government.

Hamilton also wanted to create a **National Bank.** Jefferson argued that the Constitution had not mentioned a bank. Hamilton said that Congress could regulate money and trade using any means that weren't forbidden by the Constitution. Washington agreed with Hamilton, and the bank was chartered. Jefferson's view became known as "strict construction" of the Constitution, while Hamilton's was a "loose construction."

The disagreements between Jefferson and Hamilton led to the formation of political parties. Hamilton's Federalist party supported a strong federal government. Jefferson's Democratic-Republicans wanted to give more power to state governments.

Other Important Events

French War: France went to war against Britain and Spain in 1793. Jefferson wanted to support France, while Hamilton wanted to back Britain. Washington insisted that the United States remain neutral.

Jay's Treaty: Washington sent John Jay to negotiate an agreement with England. The British agreed to remove troops from American territory, but other matters were left unsettled.

Pinckney's Treaty: In 1795, Thomas Pinckney negotiated with Spain to end a dispute over the Florida border and give the United States free use of the Mississippi River.

A Growing United States

Marbury v. Madison

Thomas Jefferson became the third President in 1801. He believed that the country should not need a strong federal government. Jefferson's ideas became known as **Jeffersonian Democracy.**

President John Adams

Soon after Jefferson's inauguration, the Supreme Court, under Chief Justice **John Marshall,** began taking on new power and importance. The first important case was *Marbury v. Madison* in 1803. It concerned an appointment President Adams had made in 1801 just before Jefferson became the new President. Adams appointed William Marbury a justice of the peace. James Madison, the new Secretary of State, refused to give Marbury his appointment papers. Marbury asked the Supreme Court to make the new administration give him the appointment. The Supreme Court said that Madison had acted improperly, but it struck down the act of Congress that gave Marbury the appointment. This decision proved that the

Thomas Jefferson elected President

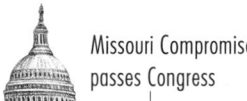
U.S. declares war on Great Britain

Missouri Compromise passes Congress

1801   1803   1812   1817   1820   1823

Marbury v. Madison establishes judicial review; Jefferson makes the Louisiana Purchase

James Monroe elected President

Monroe issues the Monroe Doctrine

Supreme Court could declare laws unconstitutional. This power became known as **judicial review.** John Marshall believed that a strong Supreme Court and a strong federal government were necessary.

Chief Justice John Marshall

The Supreme Court and the Constitution

During Chief Justice John Marshall's time, many cases strengthened the federal government.

Fletcher v. Peck (1810)
The court said that a Georgia state law regarding land grants was unconstitutional. This was the first time it had declared a state law unconstitutional.

McCulloch v. Maryland (1819)
Marshall said that Congress had the power to create the National Bank. The ruling said that the Congress had implied powers that were not necessarily stated in the Constitution.

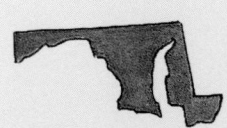

Dartmouth College v. Woodward (1819)
New Hampshire wanted to change the royal charter for Dartmouth College to make it into a state college. The court ruled that the Constitution protects contracts from being changed by the states.

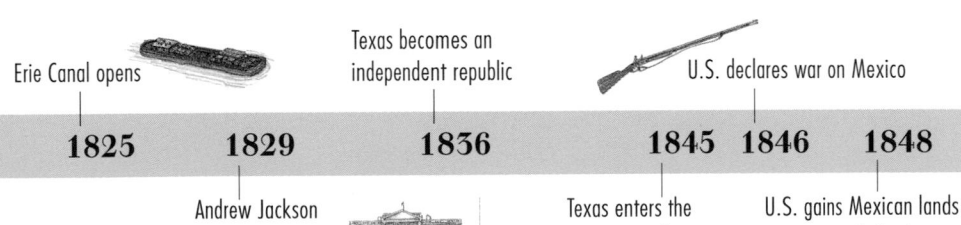

Erie Canal opens

Texas becomes an independent republic

U.S. declares war on Mexico

| 1825 | 1829 | 1836 | 1845 | 1846 | 1848 |

Andrew Jackson elected President

Texas enters the Union as a slave state

U.S. gains Mexican lands in treaty with Mexico

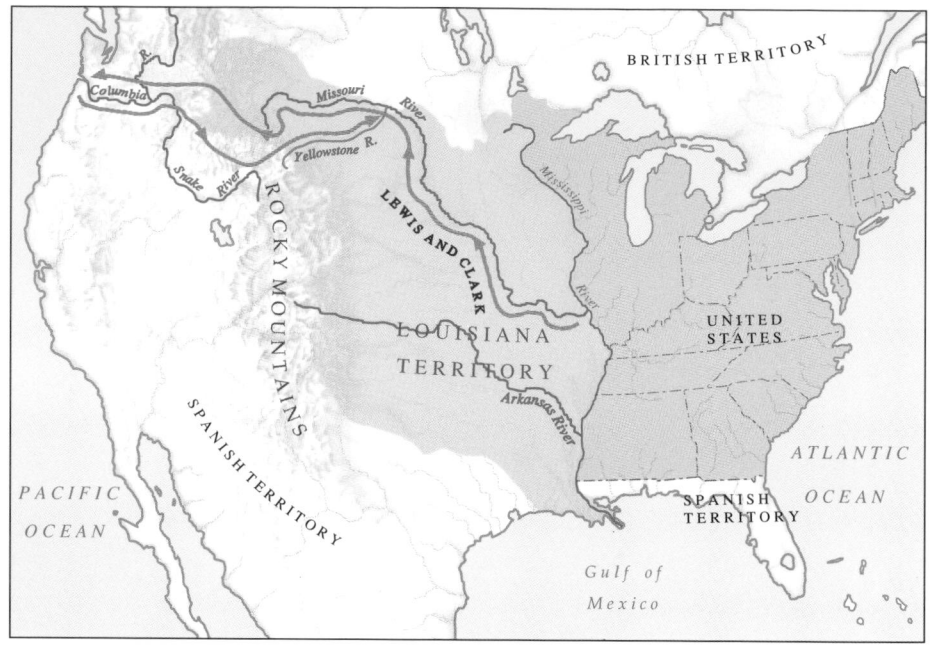

THE LOUISIANA PURCHASE, 1803

The Louisiana Purchase

The huge area between the Mississippi River and the Rocky Mountains had been owned by Spain since 1763. President Jefferson learned that Spain was secretly giving the territory to France. Jefferson wanted to make sure Americans could still use the port of New Orleans. He sent James Monroe to France to negotiate. Unexpectedly, France offered to sell all of Louisiana for about $15 million. Congress approved the purchase, adding 827,987 square miles to the United States.

In 1804, Jefferson sent **Meriwether Lewis** and **William Clark** on an expedition through the territory. Jefferson wanted the explorers to find a water route to the Pacific Ocean. He also wanted them to find out more about the territory's plants and animals and to communicate with the area's Indians.

The explorers started in St. Louis in May 1804 and traveled up the Missouri River. With the help of Indians, including Sacagawea and her relatives, they reached what is now Oregon in November 1805.

Sacagawea, a 16-year-old Shoshone Indian, helped lead the Lewis and Clark expedition across the Great Plains and over the Rocky Mountains.

Lewis and Clark did not find a water route to the Pacific, but their trip was successful. They claimed the Oregon region. They brought back much information about the geography of the territory, including the Rocky Mountains. They found out about the animals of the region, such as buffalo and grizzly bears. Finally, they had friendly contact with many different Indian tribes.

The Great Plains

Part of the Louisiana Territory east of the Rocky Mountains is a region called the Great Plains. It is a dry grassland area. Few Indians had lived in this area before the 1600s, when Spaniards explored the region. The land was hard to farm, and

A Plains Indian buffalo hunt.

the buffalo were too difficult to hunt. After Spanish explorers brought guns and horses to America, Indians could hunt buffalo. Tribes such as the Blackfeet, Cheyenne, Comanche, Crow, Mandan, Pawnee, and Sioux settled on the Plains.

The War of 1812

In the early 1800s, both Britain and France interfered with American sea trade. British ships often stopped American ones to look for British sailors who had deserted. In doing this, the British attacked the American ship *Chesapeake*, killing four sailors, wounding 18, and damaging the ship. This act angered many Americans.

The U.S.S. *Constitution* defeated the *Guerrière* in the Atlantic Ocean on August 19, 1812, boosting American morale.

Americans were also angry about British actions in the Northwest Territory. Britain was encouraging the Indians there to fight American settlers. The United States finally declared war on Great Britain in 1812.

Americans defend Fort Niagara against a British attack in 1813.

The Americans' first plan was to defeat Britain in Canada. However, battles at Detroit, Niagara River, and Lake Champlain were unsuccessful. In 1813, Americans captured York (now Toronto) and burned some of its public buildings. Oliver Hazard Perry won an important naval battle on Lake Erie. However, the Americans withdrew from Canada in 1814. The British occupied Washington, D.C., in August 1814. They attacked Fort McHenry. Francis Scott Key, who witnessed the battle, wrote "The Star-Spangled Banner" on this occasion. A peace treaty was signed in December 1814. Fifteen days later at the **Battle of New Orleans,** General Andrew Jackson soundly defeated a final British invasion force.

MAJOR BATTLES OF THE WAR OF 1812

(map)

BRITISH TERRITORY

L. Superior

L. Michigan

L. Huron

St. Lawrence River

MAINE

Lake Champlain

N.H. VT.

York (Toronto)

L. Ontario

NEW YORK

MASS.

CONN. R.I.

MICH. TERR.

Detroit

L. Erie

Lake Erie

PENN.

N.J.

Ft. McHenry (Baltimore)

MD

DEL.

ILLINOIS TERR.

INDIANA TERR.

OHIO

Washington D.C.

Mississippi River

Ohio River

VA.

KENTUCKY

NORTH CAROLINA

TENNESSEE

SOUTH CAROLINA

MISS. TERR.

ALABAMA

GEORGIA

LOUISIANA

New Orleans

SPANISH TERR.

ATLANTIC OCEAN

Gulf of Mexico

Andrew Jackson and **William Henry Harrison** used their recognition as heroes of the war to start important political careers. In addition, the Federalist party, which had opposed the war, soon lost its power.

The Burning of Washington, D.C.

The First Lady of the United States in 1814 was **Dolley Madison.** When the British began burning the public buildings in Washington, D.C., she escaped, taking with her some papers, some silver, her parrot, and a portrait of George Washington by Gilbert Stuart. The Madisons soon returned to the city, but the White House was not ready to be lived in again until late 1817. Thanks to Dolley Madison, the Stuart portrait of

Dolley Madison

Washington is displayed at the White House to this day.

The Monroe Doctrine

James Monroe was President between 1817 and 1825. This time was called "the era of good feeling" because the economy was good and the nation was at peace. With the end of the Federalist party, almost everyone belonged to the Democratic-Republican party. The country was developing industries, and transportation was improving. Pioneers were beginning to settle the West.

President James Monroe

One of Monroe's most important acts was the Monroe Doctrine. The doctrine said that European nations could not interfere with independent countries of the Western Hemisphere. Many Latin American countries such as Chile and Venezuela had recently become independent from Spain. Americans wanted to make sure that several European nations did not band together against the new Latin American countries. The Monroe Doctrine was important in showing the whole world the high standard of American foreign policy.

Another important event during Monroe's administration was the **Missouri Compromise of 1820.** The Territory of Missouri applied for statehood in 1818. Slavery was legal in the territory. At that time, there were 22 states in the Union—11 free states and 11 slave states. The next year, Maine applied for statehood. The Missouri Compromise said that Maine would be admitted to the Union as a free state and Missouri would be admitted as a slave state. Then the balance between free and slave states would remain. The compromise also banned slavery north of the 36°30′ north latitude.

Toward Statehood

Article 4 of the Constitution allows new states to join the United States. The Constitution does not, however, identify how a territory can become a state. The Northwest Ordinance of 1787 provided a plan for allowing territories to become states with full equality to other states. According to the ordinance, Congress would appoint officials to govern a territory until it had an adult male population of 5,000. Then it could elect a legislature. It could also send a nonvoting representative to Congress. When the territory had a population of 60,000, it could apply for statehood. The ordinance served as a model for allowing states into the Union.

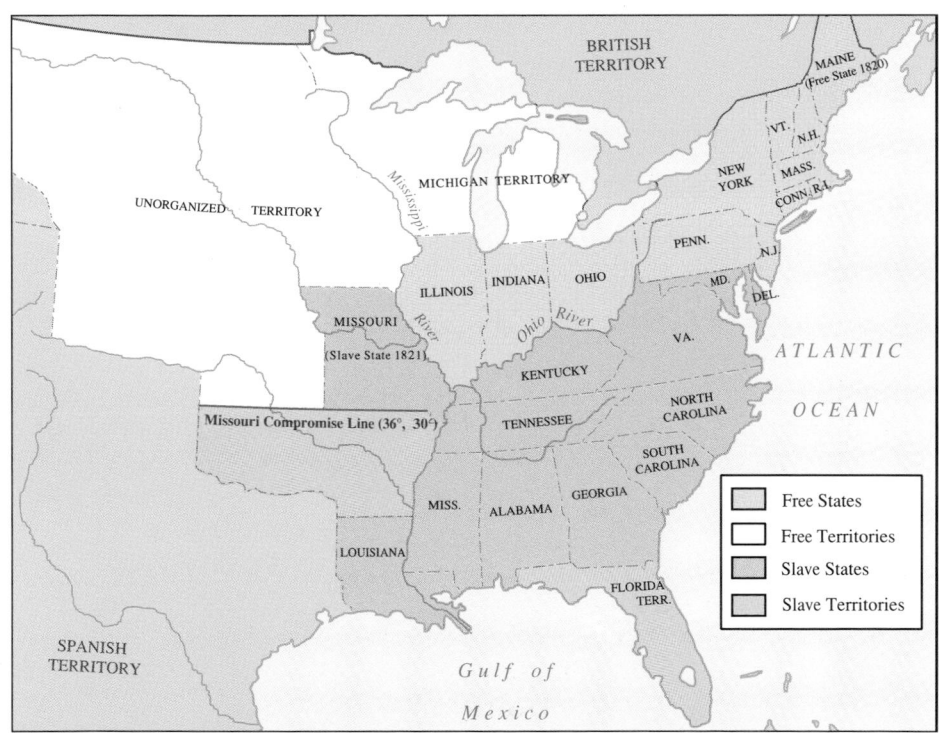

SLAVERY IN THE UNITED STATES AFTER THE MISSOURI COMPROMISE OF 1820

The Jackson Administration

In 1828, presidential nominations were made by state legislatures and public meetings for the first time instead of by Congress. When he was elected President, Andrew Jackson saw himself as a representative of the people. He allowed masses of people to celebrate his inauguration. They crowded into the White House, tracking mud throughout the President's home.

During Jackson's presidency, many Americans were eager to settle new territories. Some wanted lands in the South that Indians had lived on for

President Jackson enjoyed a wild celebration at the White House after his inauguration in March of 1829.

centuries. Jackson felt that Indians and other Americans could not live in peace together. In 1830, he drew up the **Indian Removal Act.** Although many opposed the Indian Removal Act, it became law. In the next ten years, the government forced 70,000 Indians to move from their homes in Florida, Louisiana, Alabama, and Georgia to the Oklahoma Territory. They did not have enough food or warm clothing, and many became infected with diseases. Thousands of Indians died during the journeys. The Cherokee tribe refer to their relocation as the **Trail of Tears.**

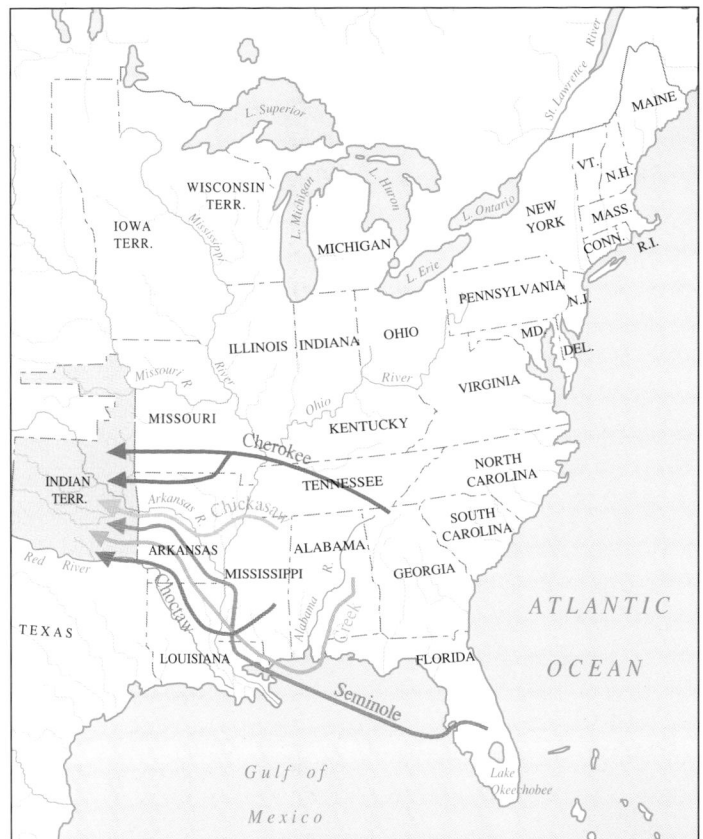

INDIAN RELOCATION IN THE 1830S

Jackson's War on Banks

Jackson disliked the National Bank. He thought that the law creating the bank was unconstitutional. He also thought that the bank allowed a small group of Northerners to become rich. Jackson vetoed the bill that would recharter the bank. In 1833, Jackson also had the Secretary of the Treasury remove the government's money from the bank. The money was put into state banks. But the United States suffered a financial panic in 1837, partly because it lacked a strong national bank.

President Andrew Jackson

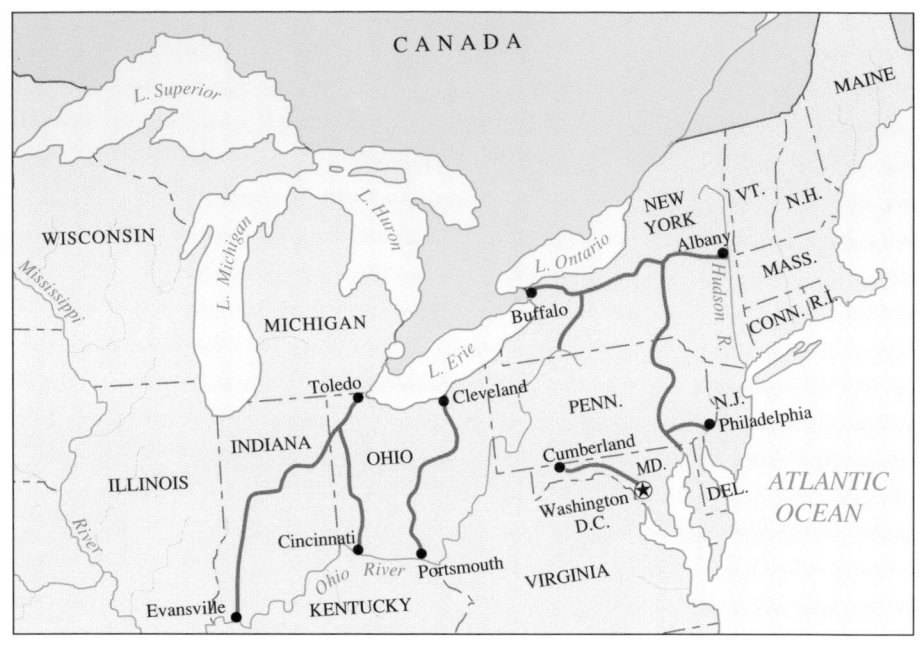

MAJOR CANALS IN THE NORTHEAST, 1860

North and South

In the early 1800s, American manufacturers learned to build and operate machines run on water power. Industries soon sprang up in the North along the eastern coast of the United States, where there were many rivers and waterfalls to power machines. Also, factories began using **mass production** and **standardized parts**. This meant that factories could make products faster and in greater numbers than ever before.

Transportation was changing, too. In 1807, Robert Fulton built the first practical steamboat. Within 20 years, steamboats transported many people and goods by water. New Yorkers built the Erie Canal, a water-

This drawing shows the *Clermont*, Robert Fulton's steamboat, and the internal machinery that made it work.

way connecting Buffalo, on Lake Erie, to Albany, on the Hudson River. The Erie Canal opened in 1825. Soon, other canals were built between the East Coast and the Great Lakes. By the mid-1820s, the North had many industrial centers as well as transportation systems.

In the South, farmers produced tobacco, corn, and other crops throughout the 1700s. In 1793, a new machine made a great change in the southern economy. Eli Whitney's cotton gin separated cotton from its seed quickly and easily. Plantation

The Southern economy was based on crops such as cotton and the slave labor that produced it.

owners soon began to grow large amounts of cotton. They sold it to textile factories in the North and in Europe. Growing cotton required a lot of labor in the fields. More and more slaves were brought to the South to do this job. In 1790, fewer than 70,000 slaves lived in the South. By 1830, there were 2 million.

Slaves and Factory Workers

One of the largest industries in the North was the cloth industry. Francis Lowell's partners built the town of Lowell in 1822 to house textile mills. They brought in young farm women to work in the mills. The women worked up to 70 hours a week. Children also worked long hours in the factories.

A typical textile mill in the North might have looked like this.

Slaves in the South were considered property. Their owners decided what kind of work they would do. Field hands worked from dawn to dusk, especially during harvesting. Slave families were split apart when members were bought or sold. Laws made it illegal to teach slaves to read or write.

Manifest Destiny

Early American pioneers crossed the Appalachian Mountains and settled in the territories of Ohio, Kentucky, Tennessee, and Mississippi. In the 1830s, pioneers went across the Mississippi River to Iowa, Missouri, Arkansas, and eastern Texas. By the 1840s, people began to make the hard trip to the West Coast. Many Americans came to believe in **Manifest Destiny,** or the idea that the United States should expand across North America. They felt a responsibility to spread the superior form of government and economy they enjoyed.

In the mid 1800s, settlers traveled west in wagon trains across the Great Plains and over the Rocky Mountains.

American settlers in the Oregon Country were in conflict with Great Britain's claim to that area. Britain turned the part of Oregon that was south of the 49th parallel over to the United States in 1846. Searching for a place to freely practice their religion, Mormons led by Brigham Young settled in Utah in 1847. In 1848, James Marshall discovered gold at Sutter's Mill, California. During 1849, people flocked there hoping to find gold. San Francisco grew from a small town to a city of 25,000 people. These gold seekers were called **forty-niners.** Texas became an independent republic after settlers from America defeated the Mexican government there in 1836.

In the first half of the 19th century, fur trappers and traders were among the first Americans to establish themselves in the lands west of the Mississippi River.

The Texans who died at the Alamo are still remembered for their great courage.

Remember the Alamo

Sam Houston

American settlers in Texas revolted against Mexico in 1835. General Santa Anna led the Mexican army against the American rebels. As Santa Anna approached, a group of 150 Texans retreated behind the walls of the Alamo, an old Spanish mission. The Texans sent a message for help, and they were joined by 37 more fighters. The Mexican forces attacked the Alamo on March 6, 1836, and all the Texans were killed. Under General **Sam Houston**, other Texans rallied with the battle cry "Remember the Alamo." After defeating Santa Anna on April 21, they formed their own country, the Republic of Texas, and elected Houston as President.

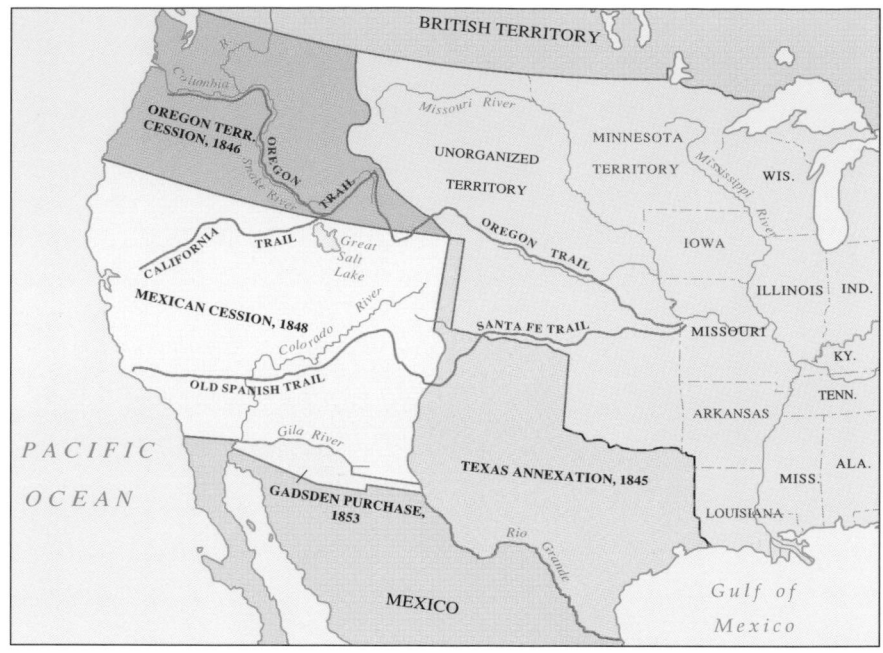

GROWTH OF THE UNITED STATES, 1845–1853

The Mexican War

Congress voted to give Texas state-hood in 1845. The United States claimed that the Rio Grande river was the southern boundary of the United States, but Mexico disagreed. President James K. Polk sent General Zachary Taylor to occupy the land near the Rio Grande. Mexican forces crossed the Rio Grande and attacked the Americans. Congress declared war on Mexico on May 13, 1846.

President James K. Polk

General Taylor's army soon took the city of Monterrey in Mexico. They defeated the Mexicans at the Battle of Buena Vista in February 1847. The Americans entered Mexico City in September 1847. The **Treaty of Guadalupe Hidalgo** ended the war on February 2, 1848. The treaty gave nearly 2 million square miles of land to the United States. The land included

General Zachary Taylor would later be elected President.

the present states of California, Nevada, and Utah and parts of Arizona, New Mexico, Colorado, and Wyoming. The United States paid Mexico $15 million in return.

With this land came arguments about whether slavery would be allowed in the new territories. In 1850, California applied for statehood as a free state. Proslavery forces objected. **Henry Clay** suggested that California be admitted as a free state and that Utah and New Mexico could allow slavery. He also suggested that the slave trade be abolished from the District of Columbia and that a new law be enacted that would require American citizens to return runaway slaves to their owners. This was **Clay's Compromise** of 1850.

For the second time, Henry Clay temporarily settled the national debate over slavery.

Internal Strife

Slavery and Abolition

In the late 1820s, William Lloyd Garrison, a young newspaper editor in New England, started a movement to end slavery completely. Garrison and his followers believed that slavery was cruel and should not exist in a democracy. He and his followers were known as **abolitionists**.

Frederick Douglass

Many people disagreed with Garrison's movement at first, but more and more people began to support it. In 1841, **Frederick Douglass** spoke at an abolitionist meeting in Nantucket, Massachusetts. He was a former slave who had escaped from Maryland. Douglass told stories about his suffering as a slave. He began to speak at meetings throughout the North. Another great speaker was

Sojourner Truth. She had been freed from slavery in 1827. In 1843, she began speaking of the evils of slavery. Over time, many Northerners became abolitionists.

In 1854, Senator Stephen A. Douglas introduced a bill saying that the two new territories of Kansas and Nebraska could decide whether slavery would be allowed. This contradicted the Missouri Compromise, and antislavery forces were very angry. The bill was passed by Congress.

Sojourner Truth

California becomes a state

Dred Scott Decision finds that slaves are not citizens and the Missouri Compromise is unconstitutional

Oregon becomes a state

| 1850 | 1852 | 1857 | 1858 | 1859 |

Harriet Beecher Stowe publishes *Uncle Tom's Cabin*

Abraham Lincoln debates Stephen Douglas in Illinois

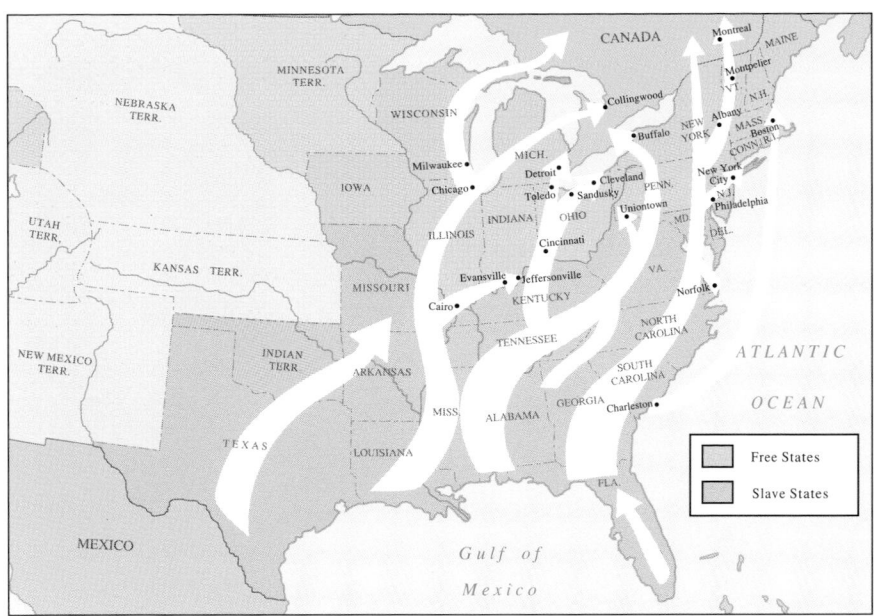

THE UNDERGROUND RAILROAD OF THE 19TH CENTURY

The Underground Railroad

Throughout the years of slavery, many black and white people helped escaped slaves find freedom. The routes escaped slaves took became known as the **Underground Railroad.** People who showed slaves the way to freedom were called conductors.

Harriet Tubman escaped from slavery in Maryland. She returned south many times and helped over 300 other slaves gain their freedom. She was called Moses by the people she helped. She and many members of the Underground Railroad ignored the **Fugitive Slave Law**, which made it illegal to help slaves escape. They continued to help conduct slaves to freedom.

Civil War begins; Confederate
States of America is formed

Civil War ends;
Lincoln is assassinated

Transcontinental
railroad is completed

1860   1861   1863   1865   1867   1869

Abraham Lincoln elected President;
South Carolina secedes from the Union

Lincoln signs the
Emancipation Proclamation

U.S. buys Alaska

Lincoln and Douglas

In 1854, the slavery issue led to the formation of a new political party—the Republicans. The new party attracted members of the two major political parties of the time—the Democrats and the Whigs—who were against slavery. In 1858, **Abraham Lincoln** was the new party's candidate to run against **Stephen Douglas** for senator from Illinois.

Abraham Lincoln

Stephen Douglas

Lincoln and Douglas agreed to debate before the election. The question of slavery in new territories became the central issue. Large crowds attended the debates, and newspapers eagerly reported them.

Lincoln argued against slavery, but he did not say it should be completely abolished because he knew that could break the country apart. Douglas did not say that slavery was wrong. He said that even in a slave territory, the people could forbid slavery by refusing to pass laws that protected it. He voiced opinions that might win votes both from people who were for slavery and those who were against it. Douglas won the election, but Lincoln became widely known and respected.

People across the country paid close attention to the debates.

Secession

In a very close contest that centered on slavery, Abraham Lincoln was elected President on November 6, 1860. Some Southern states believed that Lincoln's election meant that the North could control the Union without support from the South. Their economies depended on slavery, and they were afraid that Northern abolitionists would pass laws ending slavery. Many states also felt that states had the right to decide whether to

Jefferson Davis

stay in the Union or not. South Carolina was one of these states, and it seceded, or withdrew, from the Union after Lincoln's election. In 1861, ten other states left the Union and joined together as the **Confederate States of America.** They elected **Jefferson Davis** as their president. Lincoln promised to use the government's full power to keep the nation together. The Confederates fired on Fort Sumter in South Carolina on April 12, 1861. Federal troops there surrendered. Lincoln called for Union troops to retake the fort. The Confederacy considered this a declaration of war.

State soldiers from South Carolina fired on Fort Sumter at 4:30 A.M. on April 12, 1861. Low on supplies and with no hope of reinforcements, fort commander Major Robert Anderson surrendered the next day.

Dred Scott

The disagreement over slavery was the main cause of the Civil War. The Compromise of 1850 and the Kansas-Nebraska Act increased disagreement about slavery. Also, in 1857, the Supreme Court had made a decision about a slave, **Dred Scott.** Scott said that he should be free because he had lived for a time in a free state. The Supreme Court said that a slave was not a United States citizen and that Congress could not forbid slavery in the United States. The decision angered abolitionists. In 1859, an abolitionist named **John Brown** tried to seize the federal arsenal at Harpers Ferry, Virginia. He was trying to start a slave rebellion. Brown was captured and hanged, but Southerners were angered by his actions.

John Brown

Advantages in the Civil War

South	North
•Great military leaders	•Strong government
•Possible help from European nations	•Strong economy
	•More farmland
•Soldiers fighting to protect their homes	•More factories
	•More railroads
	•Greater population

MAJOR BATTLES OF THE CIVIL WAR, 1861–1865

The Civil War

After Fort Sumter, the North and South clashed at the First Battle of Bull Run. The North soon realized that the war would not be quick and victory over the South would not be easy.

Robert E. Lee

Robert E. Lee had taken command of the Army of Northern Virginia. He and other Southern generals defended the South. They prevented the Union leader General McClellan from attacking Richmond.

Ulysses S. Grant

General Ulysses S. Grant commanded Union forces in western Kentucky. He forced Confederate troops at Fort Donelson, Tennessee, to surrender. Also, in the Battle of Shiloh in April 1862, Grant forced the Confederate army to retreat.

The Battle of Antietam on September 17, 1862, was the single bloodiest day of the war. Each side suffered more than 10,000 dead or wounded soldiers.

A turning point of the war occurred at the Battle of Antietam in Maryland in 1862. General Lee's unsuccessful invasion ended Southern hopes of help from Europe. European countries did not want to support a failed Southern rebellion. Another turning point was in Gettysburg, Pennsylvania, in 1863. General Lee tried a daring plan to take Northern territory. However, Lee's army was driven out of the North.

William T. Sherman

Meanwhile, Grant succeeded in capturing Vicksburg on the Mississippi River. The Union now controlled the Mississippi River, which split the Confederacy in half. In 1864, Grant directed his army against Lee in northern Virginia. General William T. Sherman led the North in capturing Atlanta.

After a three-week siege of Island No.10 in Missouri, Union gunboats defeated a small Confederate force controlling the Mississippi River.

Sherman's army captured Savannah and moved into South Carolina. The Union soldiers burned and destroyed everything in sight. Sherman used this "total war" to destroy the South's will to fight.

The Emancipation Proclamation

President Lincoln issued the Emancipation Proclamation on September 22, 1862. The proclamation said that the slaves of the Confederate states would be freed if the states did not return to the Union by January 1, 1863. The South did not give in, so the proclamation took effect on

Abraham Lincoln signs the Emancipation Proclamation, granting freedom to slaves in states that had seceded.

January 1. The proclamation affected the outcome of the war. Many former slaves fought in the Union army. Many also helped the war effort in other ways. The proclamation made the Union effort a war against slavery. European nations did not want to support slavery or slave-holding states. Lincoln himself said the proclamation was "the one thing that will make people remember I ever lived."

Lee surrenders to Grant, officially ending the war. Lee was widely respected for his dignity and great military skill. After the war, he encouraged Southerners to work to rebuild the nation.

The South's Surrender

General Grant captured Richmond in April 1865. Lee took his army west, hoping to join more Confederate troops in North Carolina. When Union soldiers stopped Lee's army, Lee decided that further fighting was useless. He surrendered to Grant at a small village, **Appomattox Court House**, Virginia, on April 9, 1865.

Union soldiers camp outside Petersburg, Virginia, in one of the last engagements of the war.

The Civil War had been hugely destructive. It was the first modern war. Soldiers used weapons that could kill more easily, such as guns that could fire several shots without reloading. More than 620,000 soldiers died, and half of the deaths were caused by disease. The North and South had waged a "total war," often destroying homes, farms, and towns as a part of their campaigns. Finally, both the North and South had spent huge amounts of money in the war. The country had a long road ahead in repairing the damages from the conflict.

Lincoln was preparing to bring the country back together. Five days after Lee's surrender, Lincoln attended the theater. An actor, John Wilkes Booth, shot Lincoln as he watched the play. Lincoln died the next day on April 15, 1865. Thousands of Americans mourned their lost President.

The Assassination of Lincoln

John Wilkes Booth sided with the South and blamed Lincoln for the war. Booth plotted with several others to murder Lincoln, Vice-President Andrew Johnson, General Grant, and Secretary of State William H. Seward. After shooting Lincoln in his box in the theater, Booth leaped to the stage. Some people believe he shouted the Virginia state motto "Sic Semper Tyranus," which means "thus always to tyrants." Booth broke his leg in the jump, but he escaped. Federal troops found him, and when he did not surrender, shot him to death. Several of his friends were convicted of plotting the assassination. Four of them were hanged.

John Wilkes Booth

Abraham Lincoln was the first U.S. President ever assassinated.

African Americans worked to gain a new place in society during Reconstruction. This drawing shows several of the first African Americans to be elected to the national Congress.

Reconstruction

After Lincoln's death, Andrew Johnson became President. His Reconstruction plan made it easy for Southerners to rejoin the Union, but it did not help the freed slaves very much. The Southern states began passing laws, called **Black Codes,** that limited the rights of African Americans.

Congress thought the President's plan was wrong. The members wanted the South punished and the former slaves helped. Congress passed the **Fourteenth Amendment,** which gave African Americans the right to vote. Then it passed its own Reconstruction Acts that set up new governments in the South. Congress also tried to limit the President's power, but the President tried to avoid these laws. In 1868, the House of Representatives voted to impeach President Johnson. They held a trial to remove him from office. The final Senate vote did not support removal. In 1869, Congress proposed the

President
Andrew Johnson

Laws protecting the rights of African American citizens were passed during Reconstruction, but they were not always effective.

Fifteenth Amendment. This made it illegal to deny citizens the right to vote because of their race.

During Reconstruction, new groups gained power in the South. Many Northerners, called **carpetbaggers,** moved there to help rebuild and to get wealthy. Southerners who had become Republicans were called **scalawags.** African Americans also gained some power. Most white Southerners refused to support the Reconstruction governments. They found ways to keep African Americans from voting. For example, "grandfather clauses" in some areas of the South required a voter to have an ancestor who had voted before 1867. This left out former slaves. Southern Democrats regained control of the South in the 1870s. Many of the gains made by African Americans during Reconstruction were lost at this time.

Impeachment

Only the House of Representatives can impeach the President or Vice-President. If a majority of the House votes for impeachment, the Senate serves as a court to hear the trial. The Senate must have a two-thirds majority to convict the official. The Constitution says that officials can be removed from office by impeachment and conviction only for very serious crimes like treason or bribery.

Industrial America

Transportation

The United States grew quickly in the 1800s. New industries were built, especially in the Northeast, and many people were moving west. But travel was hard and slow. People needed better ways to travel and to transport goods.

On May 10, 1869, the Union Pacific and Central Pacific lines met at Promontory Point, Utah.

The first big improvement in transportation was the steamboat, which Robert Fulton perfected in 1807. Later, railroads became the century's most important form of transportation. In 1830, a train powered by horses ran on tracks between Baltimore and a nearby mill town. The first steam locomotive, the *Best Friend of Charleston*, also ran in 1830. Rail travel grew quickly. By 1835, the United States had more than 1,000 miles of railroad tracks. During the Civil War, both North and South used railroads to carry troops and supplies. The North's better railroad system gave the Union an advantage.

In 1862, President Lincoln signed the Pacific Railroad Act. Two companies were to build the first transcontinental railroad. The Central Pacific Railroad Company moved eastward, and the Union Pacific Railroad Company moved westward. On May 10, 1869, the track was completed. Four more transcontinental railroad lines would soon be built.

The transcontinental railroad is completed

Thomas Edison invents the lightbulb

| 1867 | 1869 | 1876 | 1879 | 1886 |

United States purchases Alaska

Alexander Graham Bell invents the telephone

American Federation of Labor (AFL) is formed

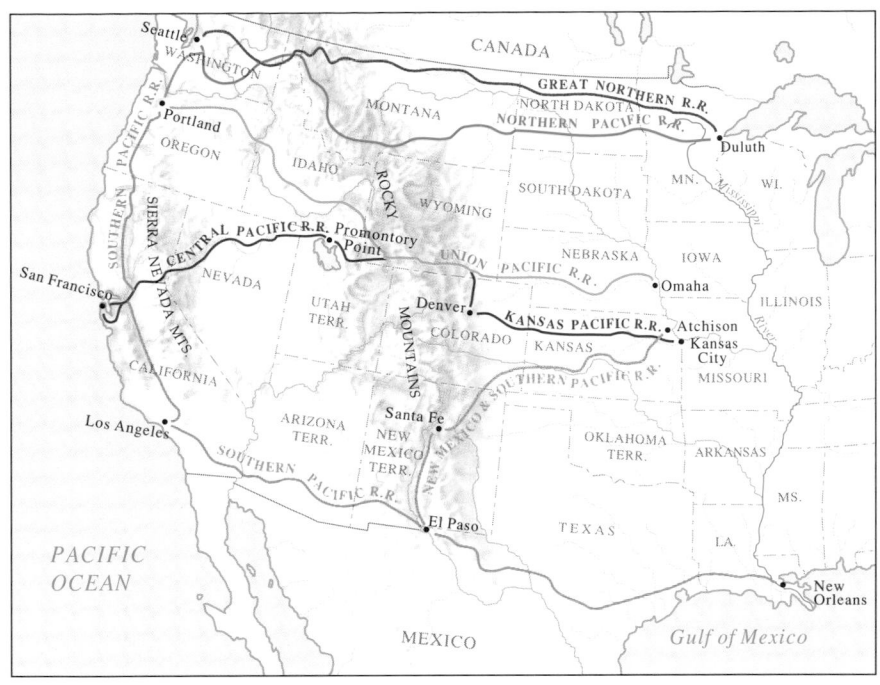

RAILROADS IN THE WEST, 1869–1893

Who Built the Railroads?

The railroad companies needed many workers. The Union Pacific brought in 10,000 workers to build its tracks. Many of them were Irish immigrants. Others had been soldiers in the Civil War. The Central Pacific hired more than 10,000 immigrants from China. The workers for the Central Pacific had to build tracks across the Sierra Nevada mountains. Building tracks up and down mountains, across gorges, and sometimes through tunnels was a difficult job. All the railroad workers were faced with intense heat in the summer and cold, snow, and avalanches in the winter. Other dangers included landslides, explosions, falls, and fights with Indians. Many workers died.

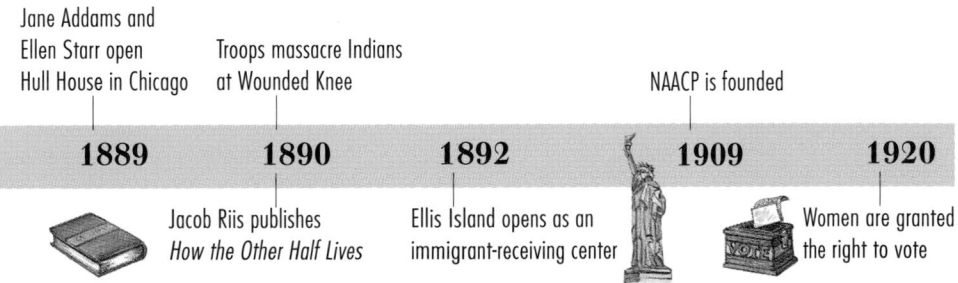

Jane Addams and Ellen Starr open Hull House in Chicago

Troops massacre Indians at Wounded Knee

NAACP is founded

1889　　**1890**　　**1892**　　**1909**　　**1920**

Jacob Riis publishes *How the Other Half Lives*

Ellis Island opens as an immigrant-receiving center

Women are granted the right to vote

The Indian Wars

Sioux chief Sitting Bull

During the 1800s, settlers spread from east to west across North America. The settlers often took over Indian lands. Indians were forced to live on reservations, or lands especially set aside for them. Some Indians tried to change their way of life so they could live alongside the growing United States. Others fought against the settlers and the U.S. Army. In the end, none of the Indians were able to win against the modern technology and tactics of the United States.

The Sioux had kept settlers out of South Dakota until 1874, when gold was found in the Black Hills. Miners and Indians fought over the land, and the government ordered the Sioux onto reservations. Led by Sitting Bull and Crazy Horse, several Indian groups joined to protect their lands. They defeated the forces of Lieutenant Colonel George Custer near the Little Bighorn River on June 25, 1876. Eventually, the Sioux and their allies were defeated and brought to reservations.

Farther south, Plains Indians in Kansas, Colorado, New Mexico, and Texas also refused to be moved to reservations.

U.S. soldiers attacked a peaceful camp of Arapaho and Cheyenne tribes in the Sand Creek Massacre of 1864. In the Red River War of 1874, Lieutenant General Philip Sheridan defeated Comanche and Kiowa warriors, who were fighting to stop the destruction of their main food source—the buffalo—by American hunters.

This late-19th-century photo shows an Indian encampment along South Dakota's Brule River.

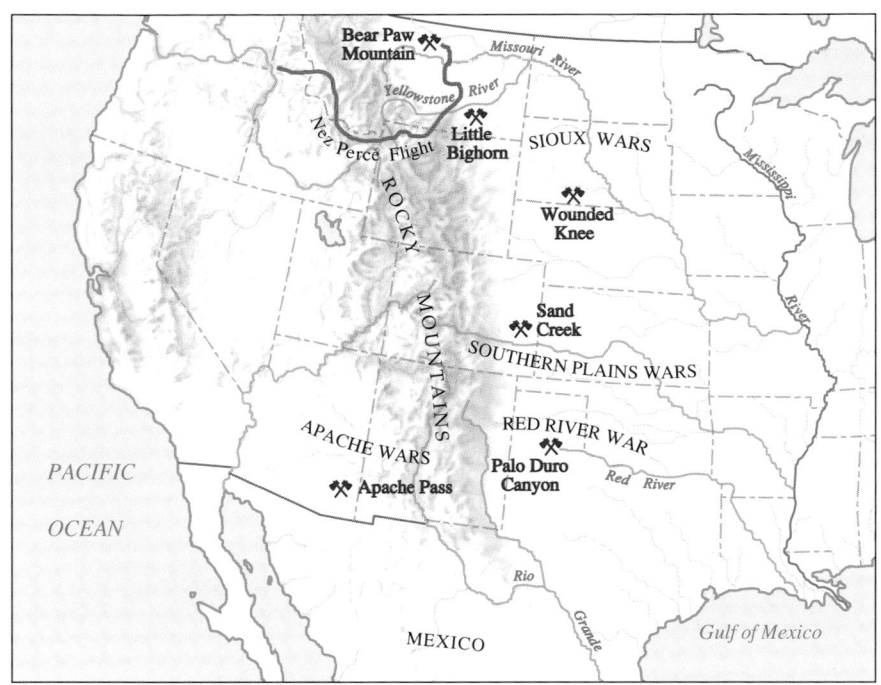

MAJOR BATTLES OF THE INDIAN WARS, 1862–1890

In the Northwest, the Nez Percé leader Chief Joseph tried to take his people to Canada to avoid reservation life. Army soldiers pursued them, and the badly outnumbered Indians were able to fight them off for five days. They were finally captured only a half day's march from the border.

In Arizona, New Mexico, and Texas, the Army fought with Apache raiders such as Cochise and Geronimo. Although some Apache groups continued fighting until 1900, Geronimo surrendered in 1886.

The final event of the Indian Wars took place in 1890 at Wounded Knee Creek in South Dakota, where several hundred Sioux were killed by soldiers the day after they had surrendered. Acts of Congress took away the separate way of life that the Indians had known. The Dawes Act of 1887 broke up land held by Indian tribes. Lawmakers gradually did away with tribal law. Indians had to obey the laws of the United States. In 1901, all Indians became United States citizens.

Industrial Revolution

Alexander Graham Bell *(seated)* invented the first phone, making instant communication possible.

Building new railroads required millions of tons of steel. Also, settlers in the West needed axes, tractors, and other products. In the East, factory owners built new factories to meet this growing demand. They also bought new machines and hired more workers. **Division of labor** made production faster and cheaper by having different groups of workers each do a different step in making a product. As products became less expensive, more were sold. Many people moved to industrial cities to work in factories.

At the same time, many inventions began to change people's lives. Thomas Edison invented the electric light in 1879. Alexander Graham Bell invented the telephone in 1876. The invention of the typewriter in 1867 made business writing

Other important inventions of the period included the "type-writing machine" *(above)* and the "horseless carriage" *(left)*. The first automobiles were playthings for the wealthy. Henry Ford changed all that when he introduced his affordable Model T in 1908.

The First Oldsmobile — 1897

faster and easier. Transportation changed dramatically with the invention of the gasoline-run automobile in 1885. Henry Ford and Ransom E. Olds used new methods to **mass produce** huge numbers of automobiles.

America's Self-Made Millionaires

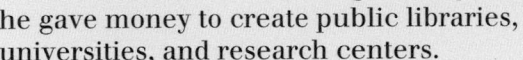
Andrew Carnegie

Most Americans have heard of Carnegie Hall in New York City. This famous concert hall was named for a businessperson. **Andrew Carnegie** came to the United States from Scotland in 1847. Carnegie worked hard and began to invest in the iron industry. He built a steel factory near Pittsburgh that became the largest steel mill in the country. In 1901, Carnegie was the richest man in the world. He spent much money to help educate others. Besides financing Carnegie Hall, he gave money to create public libraries, universities, and research centers.

Other Americans also created amazing wealth in this era. **John D. Rockefeller** entered the oil business in 1862. He reorganized the system of refining and producing oil. By 1882, his company, Standard Oil, controlled almost the entire oil business. Like Carnegie, Rockefeller gave much money to educational organizations.

John D. Rockefeller

Cornelius Vanderbilt

Other self-made millionaires included **Philip Armour** and **Gustavus Swift.** They started as butchers and ended up developing the meat processing business. **Cornelius Vanderbilt** made a fortune in the railroad business.

Cowhands and Farmers

In the West, early settlers on the frontier used the huge open spaces for grazing cattle. Cowhands took the cattle herds to grazing lands in the spring and returned them to the ranch in the fall. They also took herds to cattle towns

Trail driving was dirty, lonely, and sometimes dangerous work. The men who did it were called cowhands.

and put them on trains to be sent east and sold.

Later, families settled down on small farms. Farmers plowed over the grass that the cattle liked and planted crops, usually wheat. A conflict soon arose between the farmers and the ranchers. The farmers used barbed wire to fence off their land. The ranchers did not like to have their watering places or trails blocked. Fights, called the **range wars** or **barbed wire wars,** broke out. In 1886 and 1887, terrible winter blizzards killed millions of cattle on the open range. Ranchers began raising cattle on fenced-in fields.

The Oklahoma Run

In the late 1880s, people demanded that Indian Territory in Oklahoma be opened to settlement. Although this land belonged to the Indians, the government agreed. At noon on April 22, 1889, thousands of homesteaders raced to claim millions of acres of land for settlement in

This painting shows the mad rush to grab Indian lands.

the first Oklahoma land rush. The last land rush was held in September 1893. The Indians had once again lost land that was promised to them.

Cities

The skyscraper became America's most important contribution to world architecture.

In the East, cities grew rapidly to accommodate new factories and workers. Land was expensive, so builders built upward. The first "skyscraper" was built in Chicago in 1884–1885. Electric lights replaced gas lamps on streets and in buildings, and huge steel bridges were built for the first time.

The growing, crowded cities often created poor living conditions. Many people lived in tenement buildings with small rooms and few windows. Families had to share water and toilet facilities. These conditions spread diseases like tuberculosis and smallpox. Crime also became a problem. City areas with many tenements were known as **slums.**

A marvel of 19th-century engineering, New York's Brooklyn Bridge opened in 1883.

Many people from rural areas of the United States moved to the cities to find jobs. Other city residents were **immigrants** from other countries. Between 1890 and 1914, 16 million European immigrants came to America to escape persecution or find opportunity. Many immigrants landed at **Ellis Island** in New York harbor. About a third of these people stayed in New York City. Many others moved to nearby cities in the Northeast.

"The Pen" at New York's Ellis Island as it appeared in 1907.

Before the first unions, many workers toiled under miserable conditions.

This 1908 photo shows a young girl working at a cotton-spinning mill in South Carolina instead of attending school.

Unions

The growth of industry in the late 1800s brought many people into cities to work. People made products in factories, mills, and workrooms called **sweatshops.** Pay was very low. Men, women, and even children worked ten to twelve hours a day, six or seven days a week.

The country was becoming very wealthy, yet many families had low-paying jobs that left them in poverty. Many Americans became angry about child labor, low pay, and poor working conditions. They began to organize unions to help American workers. In 1869, reformers organized the Knights of Labor with both skilled and unskilled workers as members. In 1886, skilled workers formed the American Federation of Labor (AFL). Union members tried to make changes by threatening to **strike,** or stop work, if their demands were not met.

Sometimes union activities and strikes resulted in violence. In 1886, a bomb blew up in a meeting of workers in Haymarket Square in Chicago. A riot followed in which eight police officers and others were killed. In 1892, the manager of a steel factory had troops sent to fight striking workers. Sixteen people were

Railroad workers set up a blockade during Chicago's famous Pullman Strike of 1894.

killed and many wounded. In 1894, workers for the Pullman Company, which made railroad cars, went on strike. To support these Chicago workers, the American Railway Union refused to haul railroad cars made by the Pullman Company. This action interfered with mail delivery, and the government sent troops to Chicago. Violence broke out, but the government ended the strike.

Some Leaders of the Union Movement

Eugene V. Debs

"Big Bill" Haywood

Mother Jones

Eugene V. Debs, leader of the American Railway Union, was arrested in Chicago during the Pullman Strike for refusing to call off the strike.

Samuel Gompers, a cigar maker, founded the American Federation of Labor (AFL) in 1886.

"Big Bill" Haywood, a miner, organized workers from many different fields into the Industrial Workers of the World, nicknamed the Wobblies.

Mother Jones organized unions and strikes for coal miners.

By 1917, women's suffrage groups across the country were organizing street marches, such as this one in New York City, to demand the right to vote.

Progressive Era

In the late 1800s, many Americans worked together to improve living conditions. They formed groups to improve education and to help women and poor people. This period became known as the Progressive Era.

After the Civil War, many women began working to gain the right to vote (also called suffrage). Susan B. Anthony and Elizabeth Cady Stanton founded the National Woman Suffrage Association in 1869. In 1920, the Nineteenth Amendment granted women the right to vote.

After 1890, religious leaders and social workers called for improvement in the lives of poor people in the cities. States passed laws to improve housing conditions. Reformers like Jane Addams and Ellen Starr built **settlement houses.**

Bandit's Roost in New York, photographed in 1888, was typical of urban slums of the day.

These were centers where neighborhood residents and leaders worked together to help the poor. Other reformers supported the temperance movement to reduce people's drinking of alcoholic beverages.

Some people objected to government corruption and the growing power of big businesses. They wanted to get rid of dishonest city officials. In July 1892, a group of reformers formed a new political party called the People's, or Populist, Party. The Populist Party called for a graduated income tax. This meant that people who earned more money would pay a higher percentage of their income in taxes.

Local and state governments passed many laws that helped give people more power. **Initiative and referendum laws** allowed voters to recommend and approve laws. **Direct primary laws** allowed voters to nominate candidates. The Seventeenth Amendment to the Constitution, adopted in 1913, allowed voters to elect senators.

Reformers

Jane Addams founded Hull House in Chicago. Her center included child care and college courses.

Susan B. Anthony was an important early leader in the campaign for women's rights.

Jane Addams   Susan B. Anthony

Robert M. La Follette, governor of Wisconsin, led the state to adopt the first direct primary law in 1904.

Jacob Riis was a journalist whose writings and photographs influenced the public to improve life for the poor.

Lincoln Steffens exposed corruption in several city governments.

Ida Tarbell wrote a book about corruption in the oil business that led to laws against unfair business practices.

The U.S. and the World

U.S ships destroyed Spain's underequipped Cuban navy in a four-hour battle on July 3, 1898.

Spanish-American War

By the 1890s, some Americans felt that the United States should become a world power. These **expansionists** wanted America to gain overseas territories.

Spain had long owned colonies, including Cuba, Puerto Rico, and the Philippines. When Cubans revolted against Spain, many Americans wanted to help the Cubans. American newspapers boosted their circulation by printing inaccurate or exaggerated stories that encouraged people to support the war; this type of reporting was called **yellow journalism**. On February 15, 1898, a U.S. battleship called the *Maine* blew up in Havana harbor. Many people blamed Spain for the explosion, even though its cause was never known. They used the slogan "Remember the *Maine*" to gain support for a war. On April 25, 1898, Congress declared war on Spain.

The Spanish-American War was over quickly. On May 1, the United States Navy defeated the Spanish fleet in the

Spanish-American War	Theodore Roosevelt becomes President	The first movie with a story, *The Great Train Robbery*, is produced 	
1898	**1901**	**1903**	**1907**
The United States annexes Hawaii		Wilbur and Orville Wright build the first successful airplane	Building of the Panama Canal begins

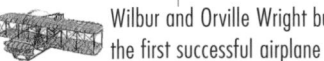

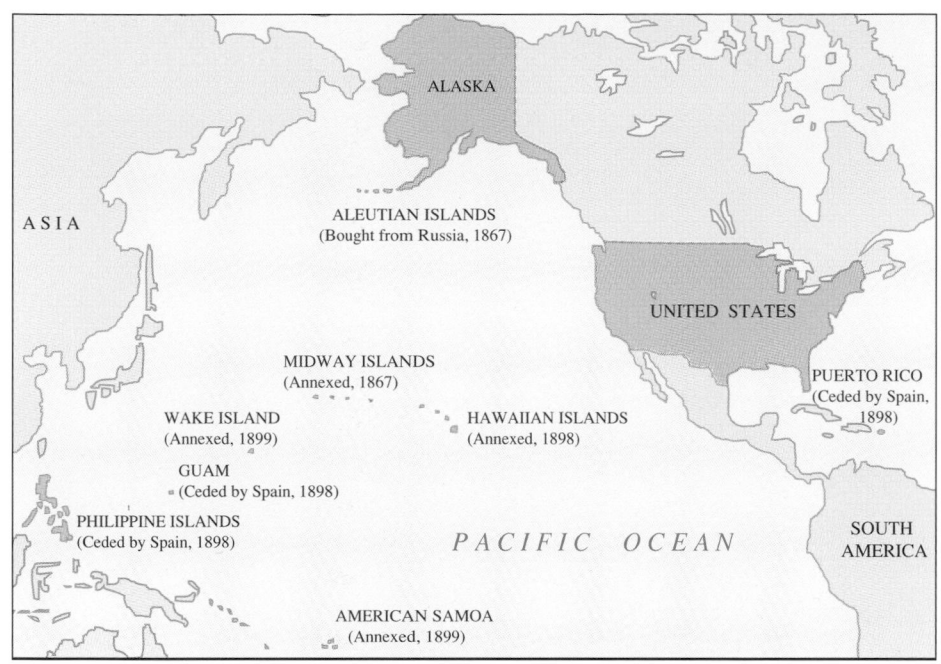

GROWTH OF THE UNITED STATES, 1867–1899

Philippines. By July, the army had defeated Spanish forces in Cuba. The Treaty of Paris, signed December 10, 1898, made Cuba an independent nation. The United States gained Guam, Puerto Rico, and the Philippines, even though many Americans opposed the United States owning other countries as colonies.

The United States also gained Hawaii in 1898. Hawaii had been ruled by kings and queens throughout the 1800s. But in 1893, the queen was removed from power and Hawaii became a republic. American business leaders controlled the government. On August 12, 1898, the United States annexed Hawaii. It became a U.S. territory in 1900. All Hawaiians became American citizens.

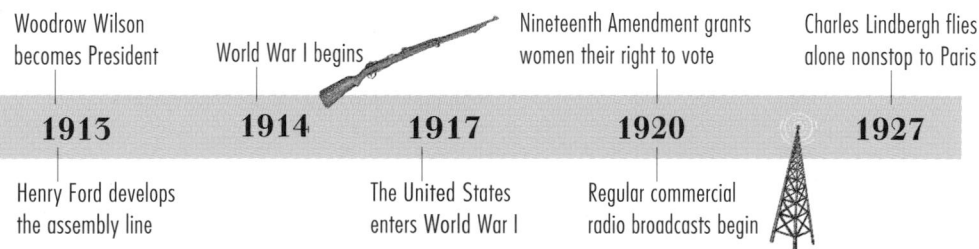

Woodrow Wilson becomes President	World War I begins		Nineteenth Amendment grants women their right to vote	Charles Lindbergh flies alone nonstop to Paris
1913	**1914**	**1917**	**1920**	**1927**
Henry Ford develops the assembly line		The United States enters World War I	Regular commercial radio broadcasts begin	

Roosevelt and Wilson

"Speak softly and carry a big stick." These words of Theodore Roosevelt meant that the United States should back up its relations with other countries with a strong military force. Roosevelt used the Monroe Doctrine to prevent European countries from interfering in Venezuela and Santo Domingo. He used the Navy to support the country of Panama so that the United States could build the Panama Canal. Roosevelt also worked to reform business

President Theodore Roosevelt

practices in America. He created stricter government regulations that companies had to follow.

President Woodrow Wilson got Congress to pass his Federal Reserve Act, which created a new government banking system. He also brought about other laws that regulated trade in America and with other countries. In 1914, he said that America must remain neutral during World War I. Wilson tried to maintain peace, but he finally asked Congress to declare war after Germany repeatedly provoked the U.S.

President Woodrow Wilson

On April 6, 1917, the United States entered the war.

President Wilson meets with his cabinet members in 1914, his second year in office. He accomplished most of his economic changes in those first two years.

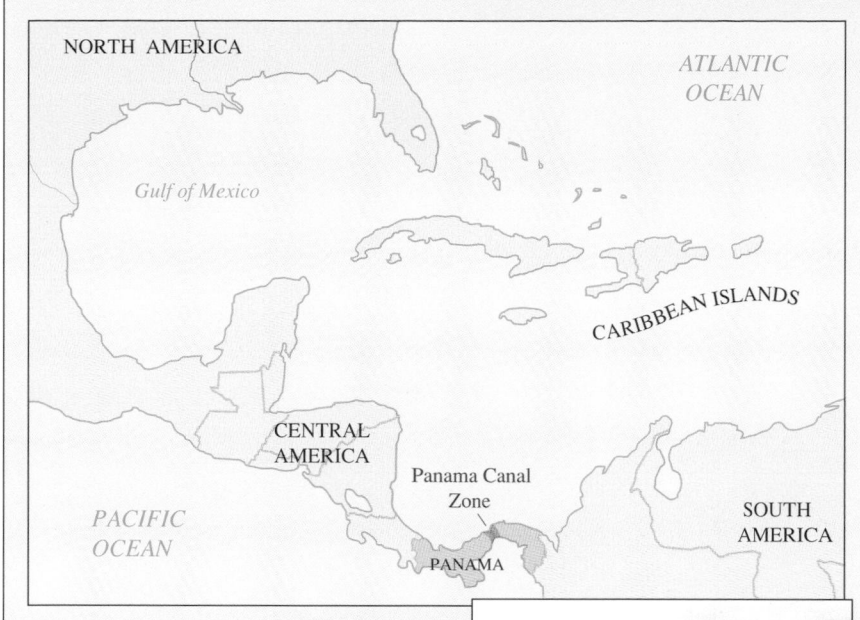

NORTH AMERICA

ATLANTIC OCEAN

Gulf of Mexico

CARIBBEAN ISLANDS

CENTRAL AMERICA

Panama Canal Zone

PACIFIC OCEAN

SOUTH AMERICA

PANAMA

THE PANAMA CANAL

Left: The canal took seven years and $375 million to build. *Above:* Two ships pass through the newly opened canal.

The Panama Canal

To shorten the sea route from the eastern United States to the western United States, President Roosevelt planned to build a canal across the Isthmus of Panama. One of the biggest problems in building the canal was getting rid of the malaria, yellow fever, and bubonic plague on the Isthmus of Panama. Colonel William C. Gorgas, an American doctor, led the fight against the mosquitoes and rats that caused these diseases. The first two years of the Panama Canal project were spent clearing out brush and grass where these pests lived. The Canal opened on August 15, 1914.

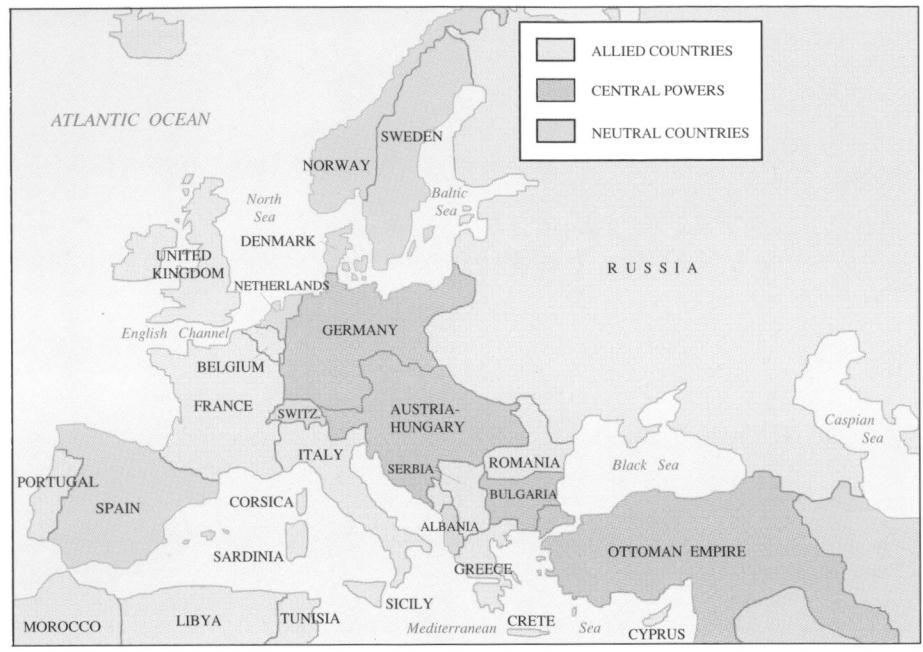

EUROPE DURING WORLD WAR I

World War I

World War I began in 1914 with the assassination of Archduke Francis Ferdinand of Austria-Hungary. This caused a war between Serbia and Austria-Hungary. Many European nations had treaties of alliance, and they joined the war to honor their treaties. Russia supported Serbia, and France joined the war as Russia's ally. Great Britain entered the war on France's side. France, Great Britain, and Russia were known as the **Allies.** Austria-Hungary and its ally Germany were known as the **Central Powers.**

President Wilson tried to keep the United States out of the war. After many hostile acts by Germany, including attacks on passenger ships, the U.S. declared war on Germany in April 1917. By the spring of 1918, ships carried 100,000 American soldiers per month to fight in Europe. American assistance was extremely important in finally ending the war on November 11, 1918.

Nearly 10 million soldiers died in World War I. About 116,000 of these were Americans. Many new weapons appeared,

The Battle of Verdun was one of the major engagements of the war. It lasted from February to December in 1916 and caused 700,000 casualties.

including air-plane bombers, tanks, poison gas, sub-marines, and machine guns.

President Wilson went to Paris in 1919 to help draw up a peace treaty. He had prepared a list called the **Fourteen Points** to settle the disputes among the nations. The list also created the League of Nations. The **Treaty of Versailles** made Germany disband its armed forces, accept full blame for starting the war, and give back large amounts of land and money.

Wilson and the League of Nations

President Wilson proposed a League of Nations to help resolve disagreements without war. The League of Nations would be an international group of nations that would try to keep peace among the nations of the world. Wilson convinced other countries to join the league, but the United States Senate would not approve it. The league did not succeed in ending conflicts because all major nations were not members. It was disbanded in 1946 and replaced by the United Nations.

A League of Nations meeting in 1920.

Prosperity

After World War I, the United States enjoyed a time of peace and prosperity. It is sometimes called the Roaring Twenties.

Automobiles became more common. In 1913, Henry Ford had improved assembly line methods so that cars could be made quickly and cheaply. In 1910, there were 500,000 automobiles in use in America, while in 1920, there were more than 8 million. The country also improved its highways.

By the 1920s, autos were a common convenience.

Another new form of transportation was the airplane. In 1927, Charles Lindbergh thrilled the country by flying a small plane across the Atlantic Ocean alone in 33½ hours.

An audience watches comedian Buster Keaton perform in *Sherlock, Jr.* in 1924.

New forms of entertainment appeared, too. People could listen to recorded music on phonographs. Almost every town and city had motion-picture theaters. In 1927, the first "talkie," *The Jazz Singer*, appeared. By 1929, as many as 100 million people went to movie theaters each week. Another form of mass entertainment was the radio. Millions of people listened to news, music, sporting events, and comedy on radios in their homes.

Families across the country frequently gathered around their radios for news and entertainment.

With the growth of movies and radio, Americans shared the same culture more than ever. People admired the same sports heroes and movie stars. Clothing styles spread more rapidly. And with the invention of labor-saving devices such as washing machines and refrigerators, people had more time to enjoy these forms of entertainment.

Women and the Roaring Twenties

The Roaring Twenties brought new clothing styles to young women. Many of them began wearing comfortable short dresses. They cut their hair into short bobs. Even more important was women's new position in society. During World War I, many women had taken on business responsibilities. After the war, women made new places for themselves in business and education. Women also got the legal right to vote in 1920.

In the 1920s, American women became much more independent and influential. They found many ways to increase the role that they played in America's social world, business world, and political world.

Facing Challenges

Pride and Prejudice

Throughout the early 1900s, black Americans continued the struggle to find their place in American society. They still suffered from discrimination. Many lived in the South, where the economy was suffering. During World War I, 360,000 black Americans left their homes to serve in the armed forces.

Troops clash with black protesters during a 1919 protest march in Washington, D.C.

Hundreds of thousands of others moved from their homes in the South to cities in the North. Between 1910 and 1930, about a million black Americans made this move. They soon

found that many of their problems followed them north. They often could not find jobs because they did not have the necessary skills or education. Many ended up living in crowded tenements in run-down neighborhoods.

Carrying American flags, members of the Ku Klux Klan parade past the Capitol Building in 1926.

1929	1933	1939	1941	1945

The stock market crashes

World War II begins

The United States drops the atom bomb on two Japanese cities

Franklin D. Roosevelt becomes President; New Deal begins

The United States enters the war

World War II ends

Formed in 1905, the Niagara Movement called for equality for black Americans. The group merged with white activists in 1909 to form the NAACP.

Relations between the races grew more and more strained. The **Ku Klux Klan,** a racist organization that had grown up in the South after the Civil War, made a comeback, especially in the North. The Ku Klux Klan attacked black Americans and used many methods to deny them their rights. In 1918 and 1919, several race riots occurred around the country. At least 100 people were killed and many others injured. Many people joined organizations like the **National Association for the Advancement of Colored People (NAACP),** which worked for racial equality.

Some Writers of the Harlem Renaissance

During this time, Americans of all races enjoyed the artistic talents of the Harlem Renaissance. This was a group of black writers, artists, and musicians who lived and worked in Harlem, part of New York City, in the 1920s.

Countee Cullen wrote poems about black life in a traditional style.

Langston Hughes, the best known of the Harlem movement, wrote many volumes of poetry.

Claude McKay wrote *Home to Harlem*, a best-selling novel.

Jean Toomer wrote *Cane*, a book that combined fiction, poetry, and prose in describing black life.

Supreme Court makes the *Brown v. Board of Education* decision

Civil Rights Act passed

| 1950 | 1954 | 1963 | 1964 | 1965 |

Korean War begins

President John F. Kennedy is assassinated

Troops build up in Vietnam War

The Great Depression

By the end of the 1920s, American industries were no longer showing profits. Other economic problems arose in the New York stock market. In 1929, stock market prices started to go down. On October 24, 1929, the market crashed. People tried to sell their stock, but there were few buyers. Many investors lost their entire fortunes in the crash.

The poor economy and the stock market crash led to the Great Depression, which lasted for more than 10 years. Banks stopped making loans to

Thousands of unemployed New Yorkers line up to apply for Federal "relief jobs" during the Depression.

businesses. Businesses then had to reduce production. People lost their jobs. By 1933, 13 million Americans were out of work.

Farming suffered the same hardships as the rest of the economy. To make matters worse, the Southwest became a barren Dust Bowl. When the

Soup kitchens were a common sight during the 1930s, saving many jobless Americans from starvation.

Martin Luther King, Jr., and Bobby Kennedy are assassinated

Nixon resigns the presidency; Gerald R. Ford becomes President

1968   **1969**   **1974**   **1991**

Astronauts land on the moon

The United States and allies fight in the Persian Gulf War

A mountainous dust cloud rolled through Clayton, New Mexico, in May of 1937.

normal amount of rain did not fall in 1932, wheat crops were ruined and the land was bare. Winds began blowing the dry soil. Huge dust storms blinded travelers and covered the insides of homes. The dust traveled hundreds of miles, some of it settling in New York City. With no crops for eight years, many farmers lost everything. Normal rainfall returned in 1940, but farmers also had to learn better conservation methods to protect the soil.

Effects of the Great Depression

Shacks built by jobless and homeless people dot an area once filled with shipyards in Seattle, Washington. Before the Depression, hundreds of vessels had been built here.

During the Great Depression, millions of Americans were poverty stricken. Many people depended on charity or the government for food. Many people made neighborhoods of shacks built of cardboard and crates. People called the neighborhoods **Hoovervilles** after President Herbert Hoover. They blamed the President because he could not end the Depression. Many farmers in the Dust Bowl moved to California. They often had to work as migrant farm workers, picking fruits and vegetables for low wages.

The New Deal

The Great Depression continued, and frustrated Americans elected **Franklin D. Roosevelt** President in 1932. Roosevelt and Congress immediately passed laws for a program called the New Deal. It aimed to help the poor, to create new jobs and build up businesses, and to prevent another severe depression. The program created many new government agencies. The **Federal Emergency Relief Administration (FERA)** gave money to states for the poor. The **Works Progress Administration (WPA)** gave people jobs building public projects such as parks, highways, and bridges. The **Social Security** system still provides money to people coping with retirement, disability, unemployment, or death.

President Franklin D. Roosevelt

Roosevelt's programs helped restore a strong economy. Their success made him very popular. He was the only President elected to four terms. Since the New Deal, the government has taken a greater role in regulating the nation's economy.

World events also demanded Roosevelt's attention. Japan seized an area of China in 1931. In 1939, Germany invaded Poland. Roosevelt wanted to help countries fighting Germany, Italy, and Japan. But American **isolationists** did not want to get involved. The isolationists believed that the United States should take little or no part in the affairs of other nations.

WPA workers in Washington, D.C., chop firewood for the coming winter. From 1935 to 1943, the WPA put 8.5 million jobless Americans to work.

World War II

On December 7, 1941, Japanese aircraft bombed U.S. Navy ships at Pearl Harbor in Hawaii. The next day, the United States declared war on Japan. As Japan's allies under the **Axis** treaty, Germany and Italy also declared war on

Winston Churchill, President Roosevelt, and Joseph Stalin met in 1945 to plan the final assault on Germany.

the United States. The United States joined the **Allies**—Great Britain, China, and the Soviet Union—to fight the Axis powers. Britain and France had declared war on Germany after the Germans invaded Poland. At first, the Soviet Union had a treaty with Germany. Germany invaded the Soviet Union, though, and the Soviets joined the Allies.

Leaders like Hitler in Germany and Mussolini in Italy had taken advantage of unsettled conditions in Europe. Hitler and his Nazi Party built up armies and conquered other countries. In 1939 and 1940, Germany conquered Poland, Denmark, Norway, Belgium, the Netherlands, and France. Germany attacked Great Britain. Britain's Royal Air Force (RAF) fought the German Luftwaffe in the Battle of Britain, the first battle over control of the air.

The United States lent materials and weapons to the Allies. When the United States entered the war in December 1941, Roosevelt joined with British Prime Minister Winston Churchill and Soviet leader Joseph Stalin to plan the Allied strategy. These leaders became known as the **Big Three**. American bombers soon began helping the RAF bomb Germany.

U.S. sailors cross the English Channel on D-Day as part of the largest invasion force ever assembled.

On **D-Day** (June 6, 1944), General Dwight D. Eisenhower led the Allied forces in a huge attack on the German army in France. American Lieutenant General George S. Patton led his army to Paris and freed the city on August 25. The Allies finally defeated Germany on May 7, 1945.

Japan was still fighting in Southeast Asia and the Pacific Ocean. On August 6, 1945, America dropped the first atomic bomb ever used in war on the city of Hiroshima, Japan. The United States later dropped another bomb on Nagasaki. Japan surrendered on September 1, 1945.

With the defeat of Germany, the Allies investigated the horrible crimes of the Nazis. Millions of Jews and others had been murdered or imprisoned in concentration camps. In all, 11 million civilians were killed; about 6 million of them were Jews. The mass murder became known as the **Holocaust.**

The countries where the war was fought suffered great damage. Many cities were destroyed, and more than 40 million soldiers and civilians died. The Soviet Union lost 7½ million people in battle; Germany, 3½ million; Japan, 2½ million; China, 2 million; and the United States, 400,000. World War II was the most destructive war the world has ever known.

The Women's Army Corps lands in North Africa. Women were important in the military during WWII.

The Home Front

In America, many women went to work in factories during the war. Factory production was amazing. For example, Americans built 86,000 planes in 1942. People bought and collected 25-cent stamps, which they could then use to buy a Defense Savings Bond. They planted "victory gardens,"

With so many men drafted into military service, all-female factory crews became a common sight.

growing vegetables for their families. Some products that were needed by the armed services were rationed. Americans received coupons for items like sugar, coffee, butter, and gasoline. Other items like automobile tires were difficult to get.

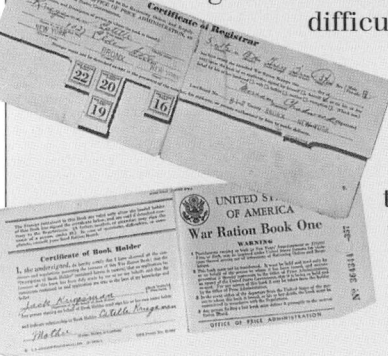

After the Japanese attack on Pearl Harbor, 110,000 Japanese-Americans living on the West Coast were sent to internment camps until the end of the war. The government thought that some of these people might be traitors. Men, women, and children had to leave their homes, jobs, and schools to go to the camps.

Above: War Ration Books allowed Americans to get limited amounts of hard-to-find items like coffee.
Right: First arrivals at the Japanese internment camp at Manzanar, California, await processing.

The Cold War

The Soviet Union and the United States fought alongside each other in World War II. After the war, the two powerful countries began to distrust one another. The Soviet Union was a **communist** country. In a communist country, the state owns all means of

Soviet Premier Nikita Khrushchev *(right)* meets with American President John F. Kennedy.

production and tries to distribute the wealth of the country equally to its citizens. Communist states often limit the personal freedom and rights of citizens, also. The Soviet Union and China tried to spread communism to other nations. The United States opposed this. This conflict became known as the Cold War. It was called a "cold" war because it did not lead to direct fighting between the countries involved.

The Soviet Union began cutting off contact between Western nations and the Eastern communist countries. In March 1946,

Winston Churchill said that "an Iron Curtain has descended across the continent of Europe." People used the phrase **Iron Curtain** to describe the separation of the communist nations from the rest of the world.

The spread of communism worried many Americans. In 1950, Senator Joseph

Joseph McCarthy displays a copy of the *Daily Worker*, a Communist Party newspaper, at a 1954 hearing.

An aerial photo from 1962 shows three Soviet ships and various nuclear missile parts near Havana, Cuba.

McCarthy of Wisconsin held hearings that accused many liberal Americans of being communist spies. McCarthy never proved that anyone was a spy, but some people lost their jobs and other rights after being accused. Eventually, people saw that McCarthy's charges were irresponsible. The term **McCarthyism** is used to describe careless accusations about citizens.

The Cold War reached a dangerous point in October 1962 with the **Cuban Missile Crisis.** The United States discovered that the Soviets were putting nuclear missiles in communist Cuba, only 100 miles from Florida. The President told the Soviet leader that Americans would stop any Russian ship carrying weapons. Russia finally removed the missiles from Cuba.

President Kennedy and the Peace Corps

When John F. Kennedy ran for President in 1960, he proposed a Peace Corps, an army of people who would work overseas to help people in developing countries. Kennedy created the Peace Corps on March 1, 1961. After training, the Peace Corps volunteers went to foreign countries and helped the people improve living conditions. More than 120,000 people have served in the Peace Corps.

Peace Corps worker in Nepal.

Civil Rights

In the 1950s, black Americans still did not have the same rights as white citizens. In the South, especially, they were segregated from whites. In 1950, the father of a black girl, Linda Brown, went to court in Kansas. He wanted his daughter to attend a nearby all-white public

Rosa Parks was arrested twice for her role in protesting Alabama's segregation laws.

school. The federal court ruled in favor of segregation, so the case went to the Supreme Court. It ruled in **Brown versus Board of Education** that segregation violated the Constitution. The case was tested when nine black students went to an all-white high school in Little Rock, Arkansas, in 1957. U.S. Army troops were sent to guard the students' rights.

Another important civil rights case involved **Rosa Parks** in Montgomery, Alabama. Parks refused to give up her seat and move to the back of the bus, as blacks were required to do

People all across the country organized peaceful marches and protests in support of civil rights for all black citizens in the 1960s.

under Alabama law. She was arrested. Once again, the case went to the Supreme Court. The Court ruled that a city could not segregate people on its buses.

On August 28, 1963, 250,000 people held a peaceful demonstration in Washington, D.C. They wanted Congress to enact a new civil rights bill. President Kennedy proposed a bill. Congress passed the **Civil Rights Act of 1964.** It outlawed discrimination against blacks and other minorities. Many groups, including women, Hispanics, and Indians, staged peaceful protests to demand their civil rights.

Martin Luther King, Jr.

In 1956, Martin Luther King, Jr., was a young minister in Montgomery, Alabama. In the next few years, he led many marches and rallies, including the 1963 March on Washington. His goal was to end unjust discrimination. But he always insisted that this had to be done without violence. King was a great speaker who inspired millions of Americans. He received the Nobel Peace Prize in 1964. He was assassinated in Memphis, Tennessee, in April 1968.

Thousands gathered to hear King and others speak at the Lincoln Memorial after the 1963 March on Washington.

King's ideas and words continue to inspire the ongoing civil rights movement in America. Since his death, his widow Coretta and many other people have carried on his efforts to achieve peace and equality for all people.

Into Space

During the 1950s and 1960s, the United States and the Soviet Union were in a space race. The Soviets launched *Sputnik,* the first satellite to orbit Earth, in 1957. In April 1961, they sent the first person, cosmonaut Yuri Gregarin, into space. About one month later, an American astronaut,

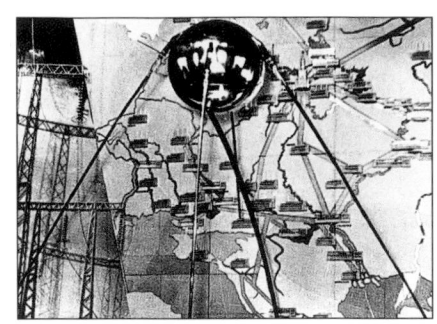

Model of the Soviet Union's *Sputnik I,* the first successful artificial satellite.

Alan Shepard, went on a 15-minute flight into space.

The United States created the **National Aeronautics and Space Administration (NASA)** in 1958 to explore space. After Shepard's flight in 1961, John Glenn orbited Earth in a space capsule. And on July 20, 1969, the Apollo 11 lunar module landed on the moon. Neil Armstrong became the first person to walk on the moon.

The space shuttle represents a new era of space travel. It takes off like a rocket and lands like an airplane. Space shuttles are designed to be used 100 times. The first space

The space shuttle was the first spacecraft that could land on a runway and be reused.

shuttle was launched on April 12, 1981. America's worst space tragedy occurred on January 28, 1986, when a space shuttle exploded on takeoff, killing seven people. Despite this setback, exploration of space continues.

The Apollo 11 mission of 1969 put American astronauts on the surface of the moon.

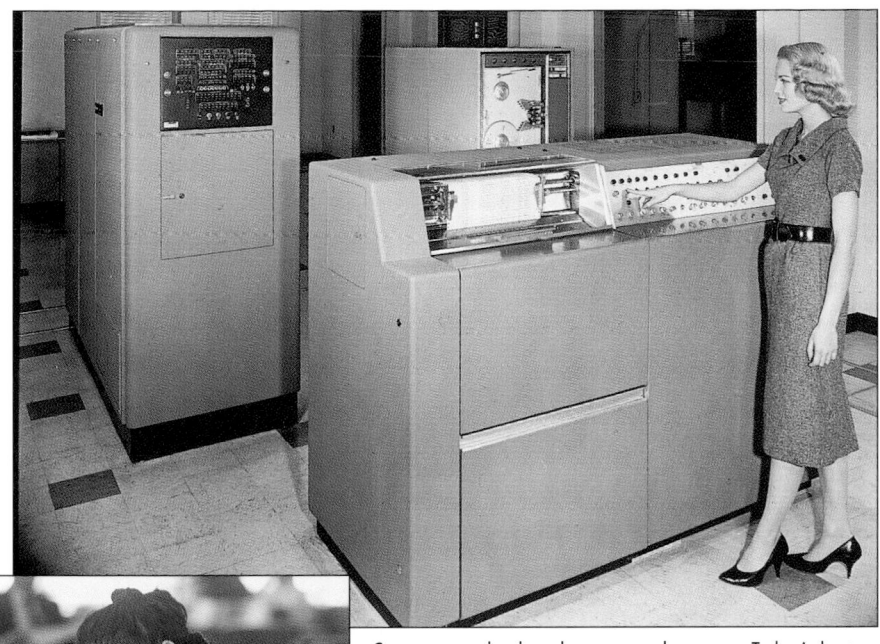

Computer technology has come a long way. Today's laptop models *(left)* are much smaller and more powerful than the first computers of the 1940s and 1950s *(above)*.

The Growth of Technology

Technology has created a revolution that affects Americans' everyday lives. The first television transmission occurred in 1936. Today most Americans take cable television networks, video-cassette recorders, and video games for granted. The first electronic digital computer was built in 1946. It took up more than 1,500 square feet (140 square meters) of floor space. Now, Americans use personal computers on their desks and even carry them around for use anywhere. In the 1890s, many homes had telephones. In the 1990s people have cellular telephones that enable them to make phone calls while they are driving their cars or walking down the street. Technology continues to develop at breathtaking speed and to change our lives.

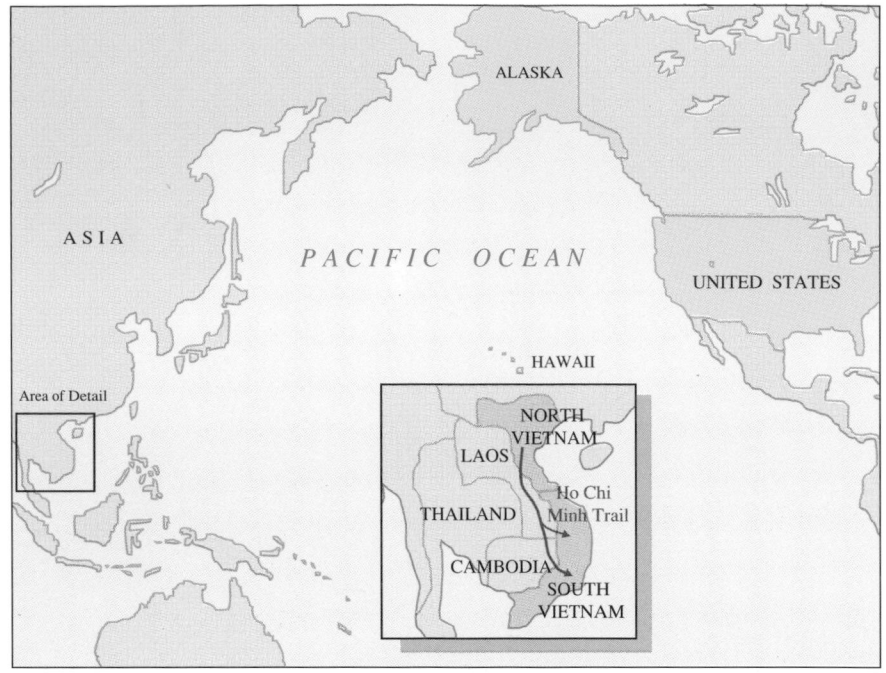

THE VIETNAM WAR, 1964–1973

The Vietnam War

In 1954, a communist government took power in the north of Vietnam, a small country in Southeast Asia. Communists in the North encouraged Viet Cong rebels in the South to overthrow their government. Most Americans approved of aid to South Vietnam from 1961 to 1963. On August 4, 1964, two U.S. Navy warships were attacked by North Vietnam. President Lyndon Johnson sent U.S. troops to South Vietnam.

The American strategy was to bomb North Vietnam. The rebels used **guerrilla warfare,** or ambushes and hit-and-run raids, to fight the South Vietnamese and the United States armies. By 1967, thousands of Americans had been killed. Many Americans began to protest the war. In October 1967, 50,000 protesters marched in Washington, D.C.

In 1969, President Richard Nixon began removing American troops from Vietnam. The last troops left in early 1973. South Vietnam surrendered to North Vietnam on April 30, 1975.

By 1968, when this photograph was taken, more than 500,000 American soldiers were stationed in Vietnam.

The war ruined the South Vietnamese economy and made refugees of half its population. It also damaged the country's forests and animal life. In the United States, many people were bitter about losing the war and 58,000 American lives. Americans remain divided over the Vietnam War today.

The Fall of a President

President Richard M. Nixon

June 17, 1972 Five people are arrested for attempting to break into Democratic Party headquarters at the Watergate Hotel to plant electronic listening devices.

January 1973 All five are found guilty.

April 30, 1973 President Richard Nixon states he had no part in planning the crime or covering it up.

May 1973 During Senate hearings, a former aide testifies that Nixon knew about the cover-up.

July 1973 Nixon refuses to turn over tape recordings of meetings where he discussed the break-in.

October 1973 Nixon fires the Attorney General and Deputy Attorney General when they refuse to fire the Watergate Special Prosecutor.

November 1973 Nixon agrees to turn over the tape recordings.

March 1974 Nixon's top advisers are charged with covering up the break-in.

August 9, 1974 Nixon resigns.

September 8, 1974 President Gerald Ford pardons Nixon for all crimes he may have committed.

A New World Order

By 1988, the Cold War was coming to an end. The United States and the Soviet Union signed a treaty agreeing to destroy their most dangerous nuclear missiles. They also agreed to reduce the total number of other nuclear weapons. Soviet leader Mikhail Gorbachev encouraged more freedom in the Soviet Union.

President George Bush and Russian leader Boris Yeltsin signed a series of historic agreements in June of 1992.

The Eastern European countries of Poland, Hungary, East Germany, and Czechoslovakia broke free of the Communist Party in 1989. In November 1989, East Germany opened its borders to the West. East and West Germany reunited in October 1990.

In June 1990, Gorbachev agreed to give ten Soviet republics self-government. On December 8, 1991, Boris Yeltsin, the new

The U.S. and several other nations launched Operation Desert Storm in January of 1991 to remove Iraqi forces from the oil-rich country of Kuwait.

Russian leader, announced that the Soviet Union no longer existed. The Soviet republics became independent nations.

For decades, the United States had planned its place in world politics around its rival, the Soviet Union. Now that this rival was no longer a threat, the U.S. needed to change its role as a world leader. This meant building new relationships with the countries that once belonged to the Soviet Union and finding a new role for the American military to play.

The United States faced new challenges from other governments. In 1990, Iraqi troops invaded the country of Kuwait. President George Bush helped form a group, or coalition, of countries to oppose Iraq. On January 17, 1991, the coalition forces began bombing Iraq. By February 27, Kuwait had been liberated. The Persian Gulf War had ended. Hundreds of thousands of people in Iraq and Kuwait were killed, wounded, or left homeless. Also, the environment was damaged when Iraqi troops set hundreds of Kuwaiti oil wells on fire.

The Berlin Wall

West German demonstrators place flags atop the Berlin Wall under the watchful eyes of East German soldiers.

After World War II, Berlin was divided. East Berlin became the capital of communist East Germany. West Berlin remained a part of West Germany. In 1961, the communists built the Berlin Wall to prevent people from escaping to West Berlin. More than 170 people died trying to escape over the Wall. The Wall became a symbol of the Cold War. In 1989, the communist government finally allowed East Germans to travel freely. Germans celebrated as the Berlin Wall was knocked down.

Into the 2000s

Many Americans today are focusing on problems at home. Many Americans are homeless and others live in run-down neighborhoods. Many families face unemployment or reduced incomes. Americans have made many advances in granting equal rights, but minority groups still have to deal with some disadvantages and unfair treatment. Americans want to improve their schools so that children get good educations.

The AIDS Quilt, on display here in Washington, D.C., bears the names of many people afflicted with this tragic disease.

In the last 15 years, dangerous new diseases like AIDS have struck throughout the world. Scientists are working to fight these diseases.

Americans also recognize that not everyone shares in America's opportunities. Many people worldwide still suffer from starvation and disease. Americans also must work with the rest of the world to improve the environment.

Despite the challenges they face, Americans are optimistic. They believe that the democracy created by the Constitution in 1787 will help them meet the challenges of their country and of the world.

Despite some advances, crime and poverty continue to plague American cities.

Today, U.S. troops are often called upon to conduct humanitarian missions.

Index